First World War
and Army of Occupation
War Diary
France, Belgium and Germany

36 DIVISION
107 Infantry Brigade
Royal Irish Rifles
15th Battalion
3 October 1915 - 31 May 1919

WO95/2503/5

Published by

The Naval & Military Press Ltd

Unit 10 Ridgewood Industrial Park,

Uckfield, East Sussex,

TN22 5QE England

Tel: +44 (0) 1825 749494

www.naval-military-press.com

www.nmarchive.com

This diary has been reprinted in facsimile from the original. Any imperfections are inevitably reproduced and the quality may fall short of modern type and cartographic standards.

© Crown Copyright
Images reproduced by permission of The National Archives, London, England, 2015.

Contents

Document type	Place/Title	Date From	Date To
Heading	WO95/2503/5 15 Battalion Royal Irish Rifles		
Heading	36th Division 107th Infy Bde 15th Bn Roy. Irish Rif. 1915 Oct-May 1919		
Heading	4th Division 11th Infantry Bde 15th Battn. Royal Irish Rifles Came From 107th Bde 6-11-15		
Heading	36th (4th) Division 15th R. Irish Rifle Vol I Oct 15 (to IV Nov-Feb 7)		
War Diary	Bramshott	03/10/1915	03/10/1915
War Diary	Folkstone	04/10/1915	04/10/1915
War Diary	Boulogne	04/10/1915	05/10/1915
War Diary	Vignacourt	06/10/1915	09/10/1915
War Diary	Pouchvillers	10/10/1915	10/10/1915
War Diary	Couin	11/10/1915	11/10/1915
War Diary	Fonquevillers	12/10/1915	17/10/1915
War Diary	Couin	18/10/1915	18/10/1915
War Diary	Pouchevillers	19/10/1915	19/10/1915
War Diary	Vignacourt	20/10/1915	22/10/1915
War Diary	Pernois	23/10/1915	31/10/1915
Heading	4th Div. 11th Inf. Bde. War Diary 15th Battn. The Royal Irish Rifles. November 1915		
War Diary	Pernois	01/11/1915	02/11/1915
War Diary	Pouchvillers	03/11/1915	03/11/1915
War Diary	Hedauville	04/11/1915	05/11/1915
War Diary	Trenches	06/11/1915	13/11/1915
War Diary	Hamel	14/11/1915	19/11/1915
War Diary	Trenches	20/11/1915	25/11/1915
War Diary	Hedauville	26/11/1915	30/11/1915
Heading	4th Division. 11th Inf. Bde. War Diary 15th Battn. The Royal Irish Rifles. December 1915		
War Diary	Hedauville	01/12/1915	01/12/1915
War Diary	Trenches	02/12/1915	07/12/1915
War Diary	Mesnil	08/12/1915	12/12/1915
War Diary	Trenches	13/12/1915	17/12/1915
War Diary	Varennes	18/12/1915	21/12/1915
War Diary	Trenches	22/12/1915	25/12/1915
War Diary	Mailly	26/12/1915	29/12/1915
War Diary	Trenches	30/12/1915	30/12/1915
Heading	4th Division War Diaries 15th Battn. Royal Irish Rifles January 1916		
Heading	107th Inf Bde 4th Division. 15th Battn Royal Irish Rifles January 1916		
War Diary	Trenches	31/12/1915	01/01/1916
War Diary	Varrennes	02/01/1916	03/01/1916
War Diary	Trenches	04/01/1916	07/01/1916
War Diary	Mailly	08/01/1916	14/01/1916
War Diary	Trenches	15/01/1916	15/01/1916
War Diary	Varrennes	16/01/1916	19/01/1916
War Diary	Trenches	20/01/1916	23/01/1916
War Diary	Mailly	24/01/1916	27/01/1916
War Diary	Trenches	28/01/1916	30/01/1916

Heading	15th R. Irish Rif 56th Div Vol 5 Rejoined XXXV 1st Div Feb 7		
War Diary	Trenches	31/01/1916	31/01/1916
War Diary	Varrenes	01/02/1916	04/02/1916
War Diary	Trenches	05/02/1916	08/02/1916
War Diary	Mailly	09/02/1916	12/02/1916
War Diary	Trenches	13/02/1916	16/02/1916
War Diary	Beaussart	17/02/1916	20/02/1916
War Diary	Trenches	21/02/1916	01/03/1916
War Diary	Mailly	02/03/1916	03/03/1916
War Diary	Trenches	04/03/1916	07/03/1916
War Diary	Beaussart	08/03/1916	11/03/1916
War Diary	Trenches	12/03/1916	15/03/1916
War Diary	Beaussart	16/03/1916	21/03/1916
War Diary	Trenches	22/03/1916	27/03/1916
War Diary	Beaussart	28/03/1916	28/03/1916
War Diary	Varennes	29/03/1916	30/03/1916
Heading	15 R Ir Rifles Vol 6		
War Diary	Varennes	31/03/1916	06/05/1916
War Diary	Forceville	07/05/1916	30/05/1916
Heading	107th Brigade. 36th Division. 1/15th Battalion Royal Irish Rifles June 1916		
War Diary	Forceville	31/05/1916	31/05/1916
War Diary	Mesnil	01/06/1916	05/06/1916
War Diary	Hamel	06/06/1916	06/06/1916
War Diary	Trenches	07/06/1916	11/06/1916
War Diary	Hamel	12/06/1916	12/06/1916
War Diary	Trenches	13/06/1916	13/06/1916
War Diary	Mesnil	14/06/1916	16/06/1916
War Diary	Bois D'Aveluy	17/06/1916	19/06/1916
War Diary	Hamel	20/06/1916	22/06/1916
War Diary	Varennes	23/06/1916	27/06/1916
War Diary	Hedauville	28/06/1916	30/06/1916
Heading	107th Brigade. 36th Division. 1/15th Battalion Royal Irish Rifles. July 1916		
War Diary	Thiepval	01/07/1916	02/07/1916
War Diary	Martinsart	03/07/1916	04/07/1916
War Diary	Harponville	05/07/1916	05/07/1916
War Diary	Rubempre	06/07/1916	09/07/1916
War Diary	Bernaville	10/07/1916	11/07/1916
War Diary	Wardrecques	12/07/1916	12/07/1916
War Diary	Bayenghem	13/07/1916	19/07/1916
War Diary	Bollezeele	20/07/1916	20/07/1916
War Diary	Wormhout	21/07/1916	21/07/1916
War Diary	Hondeghem	22/07/1916	22/07/1916
War Diary	Steenwerck	23/07/1916	28/07/1916
War Diary	Red. Lodge	29/07/1916	31/07/1916
Map	Beaumont Hamel		
Miscellaneous			
Heading	WO95/2503 Fragmented Transparent Map Section 2 Of 3		
Map	Beaumont British Trenches		
Map			
Heading	Aug-Dec 1916		
War Diary	Trenches	01/08/1916	05/08/1916
War Diary	Kortepyp	06/08/1916	08/08/1916

War Diary	Trenches	09/08/1916	15/08/1916
War Diary	Ly Low Farm	16/08/1916	24/08/1916
War Diary	Trenches	25/08/1916	31/08/1916
War Diary	In The Field	01/09/1916	01/09/1916
War Diary	Kortepyp	02/09/1916	09/09/1916
War Diary	In The Field	10/09/1916	17/09/1916
War Diary	Neuve Eglise	18/09/1916	23/09/1916
War Diary	In The Field	24/09/1916	29/09/1916
War Diary	Kortepyp	30/09/1916	05/10/1916
War Diary	Trenches	06/10/1916	11/10/1916
War Diary	Neuve Eglise	12/10/1916	17/10/1916
War Diary	Trenches	18/10/1916	04/11/1916
War Diary	Neuve Eglise	05/11/1916	10/11/1916
War Diary	Trenches	11/11/1916	16/11/1916
War Diary	Kortepyp	17/11/1916	22/11/1916
War Diary	Trenches	23/11/1916	28/11/1916
War Diary	Neuve Eglise	29/11/1916	04/12/1916
War Diary	Trenches	05/12/1916	10/12/1916
War Diary	Wakefield Huts	11/12/1916	15/12/1916
War Diary	Trenches	16/12/1916	22/12/1916
War Diary	Neuve Eglise	23/12/1916	28/12/1916
War Diary	Trenches	29/12/1916	31/12/1916
Heading	Jan-Dec 1917		
War Diary	Trenches	01/01/1917	03/01/1917
War Diary	Kortepype	04/01/1917	09/01/1917
War Diary	Trenches	10/01/1917	15/01/1917
War Diary	Neuve Eglise	16/01/1917	21/01/1917
War Diary	Trenches	22/01/1917	27/01/1917
War Diary	Aldershot	28/01/1917	10/02/1917
War Diary	Meterin	11/02/1917	01/03/1917
War Diary	Catacombes	02/03/1917	03/03/1917
War Diary	Trenches	04/03/1917	09/03/1917
War Diary	Catacombes	10/03/1917	12/03/1917
War Diary	Trenches	13/03/1917	19/03/1917
War Diary	Kemmel	20/03/1917	25/03/1917
War Diary	Trenches	26/03/1917	31/03/1917
War Diary	Derry Huts Near Kemmel	01/04/1917	05/04/1917
War Diary	Quatre-Fils Aymon	06/04/1917	14/04/1917
War Diary	Hazebrouck	15/04/1917	15/04/1917
War Diary	Hallines	16/04/1917	16/04/1917
War Diary	Acquin	17/04/1917	29/04/1917
War Diary	Hallines	30/04/1917	30/04/1917
War Diary	Hazebrouck	01/05/1917	01/05/1917
War Diary	Phinc Boom	02/05/1917	13/05/1917
War Diary	Bivouacs	14/05/1917	31/05/1917
War Diary	Berthen	01/06/1917	05/06/1917
War Diary	Trenches	06/06/1917	08/06/1917
War Diary	Dranoutre	09/06/1917	13/06/1917
War Diary	Croix De Poperinge	14/06/1917	17/06/1917
War Diary	Trenches	18/06/1917	28/06/1917
War Diary	Clare Camp	29/06/1917	29/06/1917
War Diary	Outersteene	30/06/1917	30/06/1917
War Diary	Merris Area	01/07/1917	07/07/1917
War Diary	Acquin Area	08/07/1917	25/07/1917
War Diary	Winnezeele	26/07/1917	30/07/1917
War Diary	Watou Area	31/07/1917	31/07/1917

War Diary	Watou	01/08/1917	02/08/1917
War Diary	Ypres	03/08/1917	07/08/1917
War Diary	Vlamertinghe	08/08/1917	12/08/1917
War Diary	Ypres	13/08/1917	14/08/1917
War Diary	Vlamertinghe	15/08/1917	16/08/1917
War Diary	Ypres	16/08/1917	17/08/1917
War Diary	Vlamertinghe	17/08/1917	19/08/1917
War Diary	Winnizele	20/08/1917	23/08/1917
War Diary	Barastre	24/08/1917	27/08/1917
War Diary	Ytres	28/08/1917	28/08/1917
War Diary	Trescault Sector	29/08/1917	31/08/1917
War Diary		01/09/1917	31/10/1917
War Diary	N. Of Trescault	01/11/1917	02/11/1917
War Diary	Nr Ypres	03/11/1917	07/11/1917
War Diary	N. Of Trescault	08/11/1917	13/11/1917
War Diary	Metz	14/11/1917	17/11/1917
War Diary	Ytres	18/11/1917	20/11/1917
War Diary	Barastre	28/11/1917	29/11/1917
War Diary	Berneville	30/11/1917	30/11/1917
Operation(al) Order(s)	Operation Order No. 26 By Lieut. Col. C.G. Cole-Hamilton C.M.G., D.S.O., Commanding 15th. (S) Bn. Royal Irish Rifles.	19/11/1917	19/11/1917
Operation(al) Order(s)	15th. (S) Bn. Royal Irish Rifles. Operation Order No. 30	23/11/1917	23/11/1917
Operation(al) Order(s)	15th. (S) Bn. Royal Irish Rifles Order No. 31	24/11/1917	24/11/1917
Operation(al) Order(s)	15th. (S) Bn. Royal Irish Rifles Order No. 32	24/11/1917	24/11/1917
Miscellaneous	15th. (S) Bn. Royal Irish Rifles.	09/12/1917	09/12/1917
War Diary	Courcelles-En-Comte	01/12/1917	01/12/1917
War Diary	Beaulancourt	02/12/1917	02/12/1917
War Diary	Ytres	03/12/1917	04/12/1917
War Diary	Havrincourt Wood	05/12/1917	08/12/1917
War Diary	Gonnelieu Sector	09/12/1917	14/12/1917
War Diary	Metz-En-Couture	15/12/1917	15/12/1917
War Diary	Etricourt	16/12/1917	17/12/1917
War Diary	Grand Ruillecourt	18/12/1917	27/12/1917
War Diary	La Neuville	28/12/1917	31/12/1917
Heading	Jan-Feb 1918		
War Diary	La Neuville	01/01/1918	07/01/1918
War Diary	Proyart	08/01/1918	09/01/1918
War Diary	Curchy	10/01/1918	11/01/1918
War Diary	Pithon	12/01/1918	12/01/1918
War Diary	Fontaine Les Clercs	13/01/1918	18/01/1918
War Diary	Grugies	19/01/1918	10/02/1918
War Diary	Roupy	11/02/1918	15/02/1918
War Diary	Cr Seraucourt	16/02/1918	22/02/1918
War Diary	St. Quentin	23/02/1918	28/02/1918
Heading	107th Brigade. 36th Division. 15th Battalion The Royal Irish Rifles March 1918		
Heading	15th Battalion Royal Irish Rifles War Diary March 1st To 20th 1918 Is Missing		
War Diary	Aubigny	21/03/1918	22/03/1918
War Diary	Canal Bank	22/03/1918	23/03/1918
War Diary	Brouchy	23/03/1918	24/03/1918
War Diary	Guiscard	24/03/1918	25/03/1918
War Diary	Guerbigny	25/03/1918	26/03/1918
War Diary	Erches	26/03/1918	28/03/1918
War Diary	Sourdon	28/03/1918	28/03/1918

War Diary	Velennes	29/03/1918	30/03/1918
War Diary	Saleux	30/03/1918	31/03/1918
War Diary	Maigneville	31/03/1918	31/03/1918
Heading	107th Brigade. 36th Division. 1/15th Battalion Royal Irish Rifles April 1918		
War Diary		01/04/1918	30/04/1918
War Diary	Map Ref Sheet 28 N.W. 1.20,000 Belgium	01/05/1918	05/06/1918
War Diary	Road Camp Sheet 27 E.25.d.2.3	06/06/1918	12/06/1918
War Diary	Penton Camp	13/06/1918	16/06/1918
War Diary	Penton Camp Proven	17/06/1918	20/06/1918
War Diary	Tunnellers Camp	21/06/1918	02/07/1918
War Diary	St Sylvestre Cappel	03/07/1918	06/07/1918
War Diary	Mt Des Cats	07/07/1918	07/07/1918
War Diary	Front Line	08/07/1918	12/07/1918
War Diary	Line	12/07/1917	15/07/1917
War Diary	Reserve	16/07/1917	23/07/1917
War Diary	Support	24/07/1917	31/07/1917
War Diary	In The Line	01/08/1918	08/08/1918
War Diary	Reserve	09/08/1918	16/08/1918
War Diary	Front Line	17/08/1918	22/08/1918
War Diary	Reserve	23/08/1918	29/08/1918
War Diary	P27 Central Sheet 27	30/08/1918	31/08/1918
Operation(al) Order(s)	Battalion Operation Orders No 21	03/08/1918	03/08/1918
Operation(al) Order(s)	15th (S) Bn. The Royal Irish Rifles. Operation Order No. 24		
Miscellaneous	Adjutant		
Operation(al) Order(s)	Operation Order No 28	21/08/1918	21/08/1918
Miscellaneous	Summary Of Operations Carried Out By 15th (S) Bn. The Royal Irish Rifles On 21/22nd And 23rd Aug. 1918	23/08/1918	23/08/1918
Miscellaneous	Enemy Barrage During Operations On 21/22 Aug. 1918	23/08/1918	23/08/1918
War Diary	Mont Noir	01/09/1918	03/09/1918
War Diary	S.18.d.05.00	04/09/1918	07/09/1918
War Diary	Bailleul & Ploegsteert 1/10000	08/09/1918	11/09/1918
War Diary	Ploegsteert Belgium 1/10000	12/09/1918	14/09/1918
War Diary	28 S W 4 27 S E 28 S W	15/09/1918	15/09/1918
War Diary	Sheet 27 R.27.d.60.60	16/09/1918	18/09/1918
War Diary	Terdeghem	19/09/1918	19/09/1918
War Diary	Esquelbecq	20/09/1918	25/09/1918
War Diary	27/F.27.a.1.9.	26/09/1918	26/09/1918
War Diary	28/A.22.c.4.d	27/09/1918	27/09/1918
War Diary	28/L.1.c.80.20	28/09/1918	30/09/1918
War Diary	Terhand	01/10/1918	08/10/1918
War Diary	Polygon Butts	09/10/1918	31/10/1918
War Diary	Belleghem	01/11/1918	01/11/1918
War Diary	Reckem	02/11/1918	03/11/1918
War Diary	Rouscrons Tout	04/11/1918	30/11/1918
War Diary	Risquon Tout	01/12/1918	08/12/1918
War Diary	Mouscron	09/12/1918	28/02/1919
War Diary	Mouscron (Belgium)	01/03/1919	31/05/1919

WO95/2503/5
15 Battalion Royal India Rifles

36TH DIVISION
107TH INFY BDE

15TH BN ROY. IRISH RIF.

~~OCT 1915~~ &
1915 OCT FEB 1916 - MAY 1919

ATTACHED { 4th Division
11th Infantry Bde

15th Battn, Royal Irish Rifles

Came from 107th Bde (6-11-15)

~~November + December~~
~~1915~~

1915 NOV — 1916 JAN

B. 159

I. 36 DIV

121/7592.

36th (H) Division

15th R. Irish Rifles
Vol I
Oct 15 (to IV Nov–Feb 7)

WAR DIARY of 15th SB - Royal Irish Rifles

INTELLIGENCE SUMMARY

Army Form C. 2118.

Place	Date	Hour	Summary of Events and Information	Remarks and references to Appendices
BRAMSHOTT	3/10/15		Left for FOLKESTONE in two trains from LIPHOOK Station, during afternoon.	1 PM
FOLKESTONE	4/10/15	1 AM	Embarked on transport.	1 AM
BOULOGNE	"	3:30 AM	Disembarked, and marched to rest Camp. Calm passage. Spent day in Camp.	1 AM
"	5/10/15	2:30	Entrained and railed to FLESSELLES, detrained and marched to	1 PM
VIGNACOURT	6/10/15		VIGNACOURT, going into billets. Weather fine.	1 PM
"	6/10/15		Training of various kinds + arranging details of billets. Fine day.	1 PM
"	7/10/15		Route marching &c. Fine day.	1 PM
"	8/10/15		Brigade inspected by G.O.C. 3rd Army. Fine day.	1 PM
"	9/10/15		marched to POUCHEVILLERS with 10th R.I.R. Fine.	1 PM
POUCHEVILLERS	10/10/15		marched early to COUIN, and encamped in park of Chateau with 10 R.I.R. W. fine.	1 PM
COUIN	11/10/15	6:30 PM	marched by platoons at 100 yards distance to FONQUEVILLERS and went into front line trenches. A + B Coy with 5th Bn Royal Warwicks. C + D Coys with 7th Bn R. Warwicks in L.T.M. section respectively. Considerable enemy machine gun fire, especially on village of FONQUEVILLERS. Heard of death of their brothers in hospital in the trenches. Went round front line with 2nd Warwicks. Desultory hostile machine fire.	1 PM
FONQUEVILLERS	12/10/15			1 PM
"	13/10/15		in trenches. Usual machine fire. Our guns shelled GOMMECOURT wood 4 PM. Enemy retaliated in FONQUEVILLERS about 6 PM with Shrapnel, machine + rifle fire.	1 PM

WAR DIARY or INTELLIGENCE SUMMARY

Army Form C. 2118.

Place	Date	Hour	Summary of Events and Information	Remarks and references to Appendices
FONQUEVILLERS	Oct. 1915 14th		Said men wounded by shell which burst shortly have been occupied by one Platoon of B Company. Our Snipers have had several good shots of Enemy; maxim during the night; Weather fine.	from
"	15th		No hindrance, provided working parties to assist in digging new reserve trench behind night of "L" Sector, also for Strengthening wire in front of fire trenches. Trench party was shelter, no casualties. Weather very foggy. H.Q. changed over to "M" Sector held by 2nd R Warwicks, one man of N° 3 Coy slightly wounded in villa between "M" & "L" whilst on fatigue party. Our first night in "M" sector trenches. Weather very foggy. Supplied working party watch.	to from
"	16th		Started to clean trenches and made to COUIN at 5 am. Very muddy.	from
"	17th		6 Platoon at 100 yards distance. Order of march D, C, B, A, Coys — A Coy bombed in village which was shelled, twenty second several "minenwurfen" before the pilot and our marching to COUIN. Road was shelled. Transport also shelled. no casualties. Camped at COUIN. B. C + D Coys between the	from
COUIN	18th		marched to SOUASTRE and were into billet.	from
POMMERIEUX	19th		Marched to VIGNACOURT and went into billets as before.	from

Army Form C. 2118.

WAR DIARY
or
INTELLIGENCE SUMMARY.
(Erase heading not required.)

Instructions regarding War Diaries and Intelligence Summaries are contained in F. S. Regs., Part II. and the Staff Manual respectively. Title pages will be prepared in manuscript.

Place	Date	Hour	Summary of Events and Information	Remarks and references to Appendices
	Oct. 1945		Co.	
RATACOURT	20th		Battalion Training. Supplemented B? in front Inkerman in trenches. Brigadier General Commanding Brigade left, and new Commander took over.	form
"	21st		Divisional Field Exercise. Very windy weather.	form
"	22nd		Marched in afternoon to PERNOIS.	form
PERNOIS			PERNOIS. D Coy in HOULOY. Wonderful trek.	
"	23rd		Battalion training. Fine.	form
"	24th		Divisional Service Parade. Wet.	form
"	25th		Battalion Training. Fine.	form
"	26th		"	form
"	27th		Brigade Tactical Exercise. Very wet in morning, fine afterwards.	form
"	28th		Routine work indoors. Very wet day.	form
"	29th		Everything on Brigade Scheme of Tomorrow. Fine.	form
"	30th		Battalion training.	form
"	31st		Wet day. Divine Service parade.	form

4th Div.
11th Inf. Bde.

WAR DIARY

15TH BATTN. THE ROYAL IRISH RIFLES.

NOVEMBER

1 9 1 5.

(Came from 107th Bde. 6. 11. 15.)

WAR DIARY 15th 8th Bn Reg at that Rifles
or
INTELLIGENCE SUMMARY

Army Form C. 2118.

(Erase heading not required.)

Place	Date	Hour	Summary of Events and Information	Remarks and references to Appendices
PERNOIS	April 1915 1st		Wet day – indoor work in billets. First division at armed Officers of the Regiment	
"	2nd		Wet day. Drizzled. Tactical Scheme cancelled.	
POUCHVILLERS	3rd		Marched from PERNOIS with 8th R.I.R., and went into billets. Fine.	
HEDAUVILLE	4th		Marched as a Battalion from POUCHVILLERS and went into billets. Fine.	
"	5th		9.0 11th Inf Bde Sports and billets. Selected Officers reconnoitred centre section of trenches occupied by 11th Inf Bde. Fine.	
"	6th		9.0 11th Inf Bde inspected Battalion in amount at HEDAUVILLE – 10.0 two centre section from 1st Somerset L.I. in Evening. No 1, 2 & 3 Companies in front line. No 4 in support.	
Trenches	7th		Trenches shelled from time to time. Etc important trenches, where had fallen in many places. Started working parties to clean furtway.	
"	8th		9.0 11th Inf Bde inspected trenches, and new scheme of work arranged. Working parties clearing trenches, draining, sheeting & bagging.	
"	9th		No 2 Coy was shelled in morning, doing damage to parapet. Heavy rain at night caused trenches to fall in many places. Wire & clearing. Amended – Patrols out nightly. Wore in German wire in places.	

Captain Thomson

1577 Wt. W10791/1773 500,000 1/15 D.D. & L. A.D.S.S./Forms/C. 2118.

WAR DIARY 15th S.B. R.I.Rifles continued

Army Form C 2118.

Place	Date May 1916	Hour	Summary of Events and Information	Remarks and references to Appendices
TRENCHES	10th		This morning after heavy rain during night. Trenches flooded. 9pm 4th Bn and part 11th Bn went round. Heavy work pulling rick up + out and clearing front line. Sappers work on new fire trench in front of left Company. Pulled down many sandbag revetments to lighten weight - several dwellings dropping and shelving.	[Naly]
	11th		Many parapets fallen in, fact that they can be cleared. Work tactical situation normal.	
	12th		More breaches fallen in. Difficult trench from line open. Situation normal. Sniper bright trench men open Enemy minen heard in	
	13th		Sapper trench men under own trenches heard in	
			Relieved by 12th Somerset L.I. in evening and went into billets in	
			HAM E.L.	
HAM E.L.	14th		Resting and cleaning up, drying up clothes. Afternoon Bn all went into Hospice	
	15th		Heavy snow in morning. Showers on morning parade. Bathing continued	
	16th		Heavy snow of rain. Band hearing Paradis. Bonting & helping clothes at work	
	17th		Hard frost. Band working Parties, released their fog.	
	18th		Chief fog. During Parties & hand classes.	
	19th		Much fog. Relieve 12th Somerset L.I. in trenches in the evening.

1577 Wt. W10791/1773 500,000 1/15 D.D.&L. A.D.S.S./Forms/C. 2118.

Army Form C 2118.

WAR DIARY 15th S/B. R.I. Rifles
or
INTELLIGENCE SUMMARY.

(Erase heading not required.)

Instructions regarding War Diaries and Intelligence Summaries are contained in F. S. Regs., Part II. and the Staff Manual respectively. Title pages will be prepared in manuscript.

Place	Date	Hour	Summary of Events and Information	Remarks and references to Appendices
TRENCHES	Jan 1915 20th		Active patrol work at night. Two men wounded in H.Q. Coy. patrol. 25th J.H. de la M. HARPUR and C.S.M. MAGOORIAN brought man from close to German listening post. Recommended for Somme distinction. Inwisty and prize.	
"	21st		One man from No 2 Coy killed in his trench (front line) from a German bullet. Situation normal.	
"	22nd			
"	23rd		Work on new dug into trenches in progress. Situation normal. Retrieving periscopes, & for Bn. improvement line. Been work on rifle in dug out. Situation normal.	
"	24th		One man wounded in H.Q. Coy.	
"	25th		Relieved by Somerset L.I. and went in billets at HEDAUVILLE. Fine.	
HEDAUVILLE	26th		In Billets. Snow showers. Very cold. Bathing & laundry.	
"	27th		Van Coed. Bathing proceeding. & Channel & generally.	
"	28th		Divine Service parade. Hard frost.	
"	29th		Selected Officers examined approaches to German trenches. Plan & lay out. Reconnoitred & lain plans of Hautes et fortins & work by 2 parts of men (Saulchoi Coy)	
"	30th		Route march arranged for Army Commander to inspect Battalion	

4th Division.
11th Inf.Bde.

WAR DIARY

15TH BATTN. THE ROYAL IRISH RIFLES.

DECEMBER

1915.

(Rejoined 107th Bde. 17.12.15.)

Army Form C. 2118.

WAR DIARY
or
INTELLIGENCE SUMMARY. 15th Battn R. / Rifles
(Erase heading not required.)

Instructions regarding War Diaries and Intelligence Summaries are contained in F. S. Regs., Part II., and the Staff Manual respectively. Title pages will be prepared in manuscript.

Hour, Date, Place		Summary of Events and Information	Remarks and references to Appendices
Hedauville	Sep 1st	Took over the command of the Batt. Capt Hall became Q.M. Lt Hillis from 1st Hampshire Regt attached as Adjny adj. Relieved Somersets in Trenches	Mytchlow
Trenches	" 2nd	Found trenches in a very bad state owing to heavy rain of 29th & 30th. Mud & water. Kept deep in places. Dug outs in fair trench very damp. stopped. Germans very quiet all day	
"	" 3rd	Rain during night has brought many parts of trench down also several dug outs. Three men buried during morning & excavated to F.A. L section in a fearful state. G.O.C. & Brig G. inspected part of trenches. 80 Manchesters came up to work in the evening	
"	" 4th	Heavy rain during night. More damage to trenches. 50 Manchesters came up to work. Three trench mortars were tried at Cuite Cy & enemy filled in. A Sgt of C Coy slightly wounded by Shrapnel. Our Howetzers active. Batt. "Stood to" for heavier than usual	
"	" 5th	Fair day. Several dugouts fell in during night. Two Verily & trench mortars which fell to shot. Rain during evening.	
"	" 6th	Fine morning. Brigadier congratulated us on work done. Rain in afternoon. Very quiet day.	
"	" 7th	Fine morning. Rain afternoon. Sgt Hall wounded & a man in C Cy killed. C.O. & Officers of 8th R. I Rifles came to study approaches	

WAR DIARY or INTELLIGENCE SUMMARY

Army Form C. 2118.

15th Batt R.I. Rifles

Hour, Date, Place	Summary of Events and Information	Remarks and references to Appendices
MESNIL. Dec 8th	Billets cleaning up. Fine day	
9th	" " Heavy rain	
10th	" " "	
11th	" " "	
12th	" " Conference with Brigadier for days relief settled, cold & damp	
Trenches 13th	Relief day. Gas Helmet practice. Plays put at night	
" 14th	Bright fine weather. Pryde & Hinde been who have been away two days to dental treatment returned. Cox goes to Bombing School	
" 15th	Bright frosty day. Had a great looking with Trenches. Bowl aeroplanes active between 8.30 A.M & 9.30 A.M. Quiet day	
" 16th	Wet trench practically dry except extreme L. Batt HQ mess gutter. Fire originated in smoldering beam. Received orders for L. Payne to proceed to England & report to W.O. Very Quiet.	
" 17th	Heavy storm during night. Fog all day. Relief day. Received orders at 3.30 p.m. to rejoin 107th Brigade at VARENNES next day.	Myroles
VARENNES 18th	Left MESNIL. arrived VARENNES 4.30 p.m. Heavy rain. Brigadier 107th Brigade came over. Batt batting etc. Batt fine.	

Army Form C. 2118.

WAR DIARY or INTELLIGENCE SUMMARY.
(Erase heading not required.)

15th Batt R.I. Rifles

Hour, Date, Place	Summary of Events and Information	Remarks and references to Appendices
VARENNES. Dec. 19th	Lt/Lt Phillips & Coy Commander went to inspect our new trenches at La Sucrerie. Lt Hillis goes home on leave.	Windsor
" " 20th	Full day. Route march.	
" " 21st	Wet day. Meeting of C.O's at Acheux. Relieved 2nd Seaforths.	
Trenches 22nd	Misty & rain. Corpl Bradshaw & my Bugler Barrett killed in attempt to get him in. Rifleman Shaw killed to get Lieut. in unsuccessfully. Corpl Bradshaw died of wounds	BAIRD
" 23rd	Bosch shelled us rather badly. Two men of C Coy blown to bits by 4.2 which wrecked C Coy HQ Kitchen. Brigadier came round. Our heavies active. Rain started in earnest & it poured all night. 8.30 A.M. trenches in L. Sect. impassable & platoons isolated by day & approached in the moonlight at great risk. Dugouts all flooded. HQ Kitchen collapsed. R Sect. & Rescue boys dug in water. Bosh shelled us in afternoon with 4.2. Blew out of eleven round Batt HQ were duds.	
24th	Trenches badly punished about but no casualties. Found Mortar Battery taken up position in L rear of Jones Trench.	
25th	Rain night & early morning. Both sides V active by day & night. Notice boards with extract from German paper put up & taken on by the enemy. Relief night.	

Army Form C. 2118.

WAR DIARY
or
INTELLIGENCE SUMMARY.
(Erase heading not required.)

15th Batt. R.I. Rifles

Hour, Date, Place	Summary of Events and Information	Remarks and references to Appendices
MAILLY. Dec 26th	Fine day. Batt. cleaning up	
" 27th	" " Inspected R.B. wiring class	
" 28th	Fine day. Inspected Transport	T.W...?
" 29th	Gas Helmet drill. Relief night. Lunched with Brigadier. Rain during relief.	
TRENCHES. 30th	Dull & misty. Very quiet night & morning	

4th Division
War Diaries
15th Battn. Royal Irish Rifles

January 1916

107th Inf Bde
4th Division.

15th Battn ROYAL IRISH RIFLES

JANUARY 1916

Army Form C. 2118.

WAR DIARY
or
INTELLIGENCE SUMMARY.   15th R. I. Rifles

(Erase heading not required.)

Instructions regarding War Diaries and Intelligence Summaries are contained in F. S. Regs., Part II. and the Staff Manual respectively. Title pages will be prepared in manuscript.

Place	Date	Hour	Summary of Events and Information	Remarks and references to Appendices
Trenches	31.12.15		Our heavies bombarded enemy front line. Fine morning, wet afternoon. HILLIS returned. Received orders to relieve 14th Ry.	7th
"	1.1.16		Still a rest. Bank very heavy at 11.10 pm (Incidentally midnight until 12am) Rapid fire, MGs & trench Mortars. 31.1.15	7th
VARRENNES	2.1.16		Wet day. Bath, cleaning up.	7th
"	3.1.16		Relief day mean delta. Relief ended the tin convulsion at 8 pm, 10 pm & 1 am. No damage (excepting 1 man slightly Done daz)	7th
Trenches	4.1.16		Our Artillery bombarded Quadrilateral front trenches & cut wire with 18 pounders, 4.2 & 9.3 guns. Very great damage done to Bosch Trenches. In the afternoon the North Wall of HAMMEL on our right	7th
"	5.1.16		Fine day. Heavy retaliation by our guns for the HAMMEL bombardment. 6g reliefs. 2 men wounded	7th
"	6.1.16		Still much rain. Rainy fire with trenches. Quiet night. Handed over to MAJOR EWART & went on leave.	7th
"	7.1.16		Relief day. Very quiet. Rain off & on.	7th
MAILLY	8.1.16		Fine, cleaning up.	7th
"	9.1.16		" " " Col. & visited Bouzincourt.	7th
"	10.1.16		Fine. C in C visited Brigade H Q & presented with Billets.	7th
"	11.1.16		Relief day. Three trench mortars & rifle grenades on Redan. Showers	7th
"	12.1.16		Busy for camps. Three trench mortars. Fired white rockets at 7 pm. Fine	7th
"	13.1.16		Fine. Very quiet all day.	7th
"	14.1.16		HILLIS (Lieut & Adj) wounded. Bosch shelled us very heavily at 2.30 am for ten minutes.	7th

Army Form C. 2118.

WAR DIARY
or
INTELLIGENCE SUMMARY.   15th R.I. Rifles

(Erase heading not required.)

Instructions regarding War Diaries and Intelligence Summaries are contained in F.S. Regs., Part II. and the Staff Manual respectively. Title pages will be prepared in manuscript.

Place	Date	Hour	Summary of Events and Information	Remarks and references to Appendices
Trenches	15.1.16		Relief with 9th R.I. Rifles completed 7.7.20. Very quiet. Showers	7.1.4
VARRENNES	16.1.16		Cleaning up. Patrols over tramway on return from leave. Showers	7.1.4
"	17.1.16		" Snow storm	7.1.4
"	18.1.16		Rest day	7.1.4
"	19.1.16		Tour relief. Both sides prisoners of CRATER dump rifles but without enter party on road at	7.1.4
Trenches	20.1.16		Fane a party of Duke of Wellington's Regt. Sniped & one of our men killed by rifle grenade. 8.45 PM. Enemy party of about 30 attacked & bombed CRATER. We drove them off by rifle & machine gun fire. One sentry wounded one wounded & missing of the Mont verres affected. Retaliated with Howis & T.M. battery	7.1.4
"	21.1.16		Very quiet. Fine	7.1.4
"	22.1.16		Very heavy shelling all morning by enemy. Bosche shelled trenches & REDAN Casualties killed 3 wounded	7.1.4
"	23.1.16		Relief day. Quiet. Bosch shelled TENDERLOIN with a few shrapnel all short	7.1.4
MAILLY	24.1.16		Fine. Cleaning up	7.1.4
"	25.1.16		Fine. Funeral of Lieut. Vinta Mailly Section at Corps H.Q.	7.1.4
"	26.1.16		" On casualty during working party	7.1.4
"	27.1.16		Fine. Pale ofter day. Light fire in a bullet. Gas alarm about 8 P.M. passed down from 48th Div & 36th Div of 7	7.1.4
Trenches	28.1.16		Fog. Gas alarm from 48th & 37th divisions at 7.35 A.M.	7.1.4

Army Form C. 2118.

WAR DIARY
or
INTELLIGENCE SUMMARY.
(Erase heading not required.)

Instructions regarding War Diaries and Intelligence Summaries are contained in F. S. Regs., Part II. and the Staff Manual respectively. Title pages will be prepared in manuscript.

Place	Date	Hour	Summary of Events and Information	Remarks and references to Appendices
Trenches	29.1.16		GAS alarm from Division on Right at 7.20AM. Very quiet day & night except at Stand To when Bosch put a quantity of Rifle grenades over in usual traverses. & Shelled pt J trench & TENDERLOIN with Shrapnel. He also shelled the SUCRERIE & AUCHONVILLIERS with Rif.	July.
"	30.1.16		Quiet morning. Very Foggy early. clear & fine later. Wind S.S.W. To N.NE.	July. July. July.

15ᵗʰ R. Irish Rif.
36ᵗʰ Div

Vol. 5

rejoined XXXV ᵗʰ DIVᶠ
Feb 7

WAR DIARY
or
INTELLIGENCE SUMMARY

Army Form C. 2118.

15th R. 1 Rifles

Place	Date	Hour	Summary of Events and Information	Remarks and references to Appendices
TRENCHES	31.1.16		Fine but dull. Bosch shelled REDAN 1PM to 1:30pm & again at 3:30pm Fy. Our heavies replied at 2:30 P.M.	July
VARRENES	1.2.16		Shelled TENDERLOIN. Our casualties three killed & one wounded. W.Riding Reg. two killed & 2 wounded. Relieved.	July
"	2.2.16		Fine day cleaning up	July
"	3.2.16		Fine	July
"	4.2.16		Few Lieut Brown reported	July
TRENCHES	5.2.16		Dull & wet. Gen Houlton came over to say goodbye. Relief night	July
"	6.2.16		Fine clear day. Brig Gen came round Trenches. Some shelling & rifle grenade work. One killed & two wounded.	July
"	7.2.16		Fine. Bosch shelled fairly heavily. A lot of Duds. Also wet trench mortars two one of which more Duds	July
"	8.2.16		Fine day wet night	July
MAILLY	9.2.16		Gen. Gen & Brig Gen came round. TENDERLOIN shelled. Great accumulation of sand bags. No casualties. Relief night	July
"	10.2.16		Fine cleaning up. Sir H Raphael Lt MP attached for notes	July
"	11.2.16		Hot of As. inspected billets. Common Cantuse. La Fine slight Snow.	July
"	12.2.16		Wet G.O.C. inspected billets. Sir H Raphael left for England	July
TRENCHES	13.2.16		Relief. Had a arrival by of 10th R. Innis Fus attached for instruction. Quiet night	July
"	14.2.16		Showers. Fires Ld. Very wet night. R.A. shelled 70 71 from 10AM to 11AM Good results. Left for cover at a FLEXICOURT	July
"			Shower & wet afternoon. 17th Corps Commander visited trenches	July

1577 Wt.W10791/1773 500,000 7/15 D.D. & L. A.D.S.S./Forms/C. 2118.

WAR DIARY or INTELLIGENCE SUMMARY.

Army Form C. 2118.

15th R. I. Rifles

(Erase heading not required.)

Place	Date	Hour	Summary of Events and Information	Remarks and references to Appendices
TRENCHES	15.2.16		G.O.C. + Brig. visited 109th Brigade visited trenches	7th
	16.2.16		Relief day. Very wet all day. R.A. shelled BEAUMONT HAMEL	7th
BEAUSSART	17.2.16		Heavy rain all day	7th
"	18.2.16		Wet afternoon. Usual working parties	7th
"	19.2.16		Usual working parties. Boch attempted cutting out. Very heavy artillery on both sides	7th
"	20.2.16		Relief night. During relief Bosh trench mortared REDAN. 14 casualties 3 killed. Quiet night	7th
TRENCHES	21.2.16		Weather fine. Quiet day & night	7th
	22.2.16		Fine morning. Snow later. C.O. returned. Very quiet	7th
	23.2.16		More Snow. Quiet day & night. Seven men wounded. Our snipers claimed to kill 9.O.C. Bosh company	7th
	24.2.16		Very Fine. R.A shelled HAMEL relief en route 10th R.I. Fus. Very quiet	7th
ACHEUX	25.2.16		Snow Fatigues	7th
ACHEUX	26.2.16		" " "	7th
	27.2.16		" Fine "	7th
	28.2.16		" " "	7th
	29.2.16		Moved to MAILLY to fatigues on mine zone	7th
MAILLY	1.3.16		MAILLY fatigues wet	7th

Army Form C. 2118.

WAR DIARY
or
INTELLIGENCE SUMMARY.
(Erase heading not required.)

15th (S.) Bn. R. Ir. Rifles.

15th Bn. R. I. Rifles 115/

Place	Date	Hour	Summary of Events and Information	Remarks and references to Appendices
MAILLY	2.3.16		In Billets. Wet day	764
"	3.3.16		Fine. Relieved 11th R. I. Fus.	764
Trenches	4.3.16		Snow all day. Very quiet	764
"	5.3.16		Fine frosty morning. Enemy shelled REDAN intermittently all day & our transport in the evening	764
"	6.3.16		Snow early morning then fine. At 8.30 pm enemy opened bombardment & sent over rifle grenades & mining 5.9 on R.G.y Front line, CHATHAM Tr. & AVENUE & TENDERLOIN. Also trench mortars to 15 mins. Also shelled AUCHONVILLERS & outskirts of MAILLY. All communication except by runners cut between BATT. H.Q. Brigade & R.G.y H.Q. Casualties two own wounded & one concussed. At 9 pm they had another 20.T. & Trench Mortar burst of fire trained on the REDAN	764
"	7.3.16		Relief. V. quiet	764
BEAUSSART	8.3.16		Snow. Very cold.	764
"	9.3.16		Very cold.	764
"	10.3.16		" Heavy stuff on our R. at 1 AM. Between R.G. 36th Div. & L.G. next Div.	764
"	11.3.16		Relief. V. quiet	764
Trenches	12.3.16		Lovely morning. Did a great deal of sniping in view of going to REDAN. Bright moon	764
"	13.3.16		" Enemy shelled R.G.y at 10.15 AM & brought down one Boxer plane behind SERRE. V. busy putting out wire	764
"	14.3.16		Lovely morning. Enemy plane over TENDERLOIN	764

Army Form C. 2118.

WAR DIARY
or
INTELLIGENCE SUMMARY.

(Erase heading not required.)

18th (S.) Bn. R. Ir. Rifles.

Instructions regarding War Diaries and Intelligence Summaries are contained in F. S. Regs., Part II. and the Staff Manual respectively. Title pages will be prepared in manuscript.

Place	Date	Hour	Summary of Events and Information	Remarks and references to Appendices
Trenches	15.3.16		Lovely day. Relief with 9th R.I.R. 2nd Lieut Hogg went sick.	July
BEAUSSART	16.3.16		Lovely day. Inspection Parade in afternoon.	July
"	17.3.16		" Transport horses Lieut Knight in hospital	July
"	18.3.16		"	July
"	19.3.16		" Parade at 6.30 AM	July
"	20.3.16		" Two Coys roped driving	July
"	21.3.16		Dull Relief quiet	July
Trenches	22.3.16		Dull Enemy exploded a mine upon appearance of Crater blew in our gallery. No damage to us	July
"	23.3.16		Fine but dull quiet. Six officers & 20 N.C.O. 31st Div arrive for instruction	July
"	24.3.16		Improved. A further Six officers & 20 NCOs reported for daily instruction	July
"	25.3.16		Fine Enemy day. Brenches & duty. Lt. Barnard of Brigadier came up.	July
"	26.3.16		Wet morning. Fine but dull later. V quiet	July
"	27.3.16		Fine morning. Relief day	July
BEAUSSART	28.3.16		Fine. Relieved by 31st Division. Very windy & squalls in afternoon & evening	July
VARENNES	29.3.16		Fine. Coys under Coy officers. Heavy snow afternoon	July
"	30.3.16		Fine. Coys under Coy officers & Specialists morning. Route March afternoon	July

15 R Ind Rifles
Vol 6

Army Form C. 2118.

WAR DIARY
or
INTELLIGENCE SUMMARY.
(Erase heading not required.)

15th R. I. Rifles

Instructions regarding War Diaries and Intelligence Summaries are contained in F.S. Regs., Part II. and the Staff Manual respectively. Title pages will be prepared in manuscript.

15th. (S.) Bn. R. I. Rifles

Place	Date	Hour	Summary of Events and Information	Remarks and references to Appendices
VARENNES	31.3.16		Lovely day. Coy work. Gas demonstration	J44
"	1.4.16		Fine "	J44
"	2.4.16		Fine Church Parade & inspection of Billets	J44
"	3.4.16		Fine 350 men on working parties	J44
"	4.4.16		Shower Working parties & Coy work	J44
"	5.4.16		Lovely day 480 men on working parties	J44
"	6.4.16		" "	J44
"	7.4.16		" " Coy	J44
"	8.4.16		" " Route march	J44
"	9.4.16		" " Church Parade & inspection of Billets	J44
"	10.4.16		" " Coy work	J44
"	11.4.16		Heavy showers all day Coy work	J44
"	12.4.16		" "	J44
"	13.4.16		" " morning Route march	J44
"	14.4.16		" " Coy work	J44
"	15.4.16		Hail showers " "	J44

Army Form C. 2118.

WAR DIARY
or
INTELLIGENCE SUMMARY.
(Erase heading not required.)

XXXVI

15th R.I. Rifles Vol 7

15th (S.) Bn. R. Ir. Rifles.

Place	Date	Hour	Summary of Events and Information	Remarks and references to Appendices
VARENNES	16.4.16		Lovely day. Church Parade & inspection of Billets	749
"	17.4.16		Rain	749
"	18.4.16		Visited practice trenches. Wet & blowing hard	749
"	19.4.16		Very wet day. Inspected Transport lines	749
"	20.4.16		Showery. Visited practice trenches with Brigadier	749
"	21.4.16		Wet day	749
"	22.4.16		" " Col. & adj. inspected practice trenches	749
"	23.4.16		Same " Church Parade & Billet inspection. Conference at Brigade in afternoon	749
"	24.4.16		" Holiday. Battn Sports	749
"	25.4.16		Very Hot day. Battn seeing over practice trenches	749
"	26.4.16		" " Battn finding all Brigade fatigues. Officers(not employed) studying trench warfare	749
"	27.4.16		" " " "	749
"	28.4.16		" " " "	749
"	29.4.16		" " Battn on practice trenches	749
"	30.4.16		" " Church parade & Billet Inspection afternoon	749

WAR DIARY
or
INTELLIGENCE SUMMARY.
(Erase heading not required.)

Army Form C. 2118.

XXXVI
15th R/Rifles Vol 8

Place	Date	Hour	Summary of Events and Information	Remarks and references to Appendices
VARRENES	1.5.16		Fine & v hot Batt on Practice Trenches	7/4
	2.5.16		Thunder Shower " " " "	7/4
	3.5.16		Fine & cool " " " "	7/4
	4.5.16		Hot & fine Brigade day " " "	7/4
	5.5.16		Very Hot Batt " " "	7/4
	6.5.16		" " Coy work	7/4
FORCEVILLE	7.5.16		Fine day moved half Batt & HQ to Forceville & half Batt to HEDAUVILLE	7/4
	8.5.16		" " Batt on working parties	7/4
	9.5.16		Wet " " " "	7/4
	10.5.16		Fine " " " "	7/4
	11.5.16		" " " " " Officers visited front line trenches of our sector	7/4
	12.5.16		" " " " "	7/4
	13.5.16		" " " " "	7/4
	14.5.16		" " " " "	7/4
	15.5.16		" " " " "	7/4
	16.5.16		" " " " "	7/4

WAR DIARY
or
INTELLIGENCE SUMMARY.   15th R. I. Rifles

(Erase heading not required.)

Army Form C. 2118.

Place	Date	Hour	Summary of Events and Information	Remarks and references to Appendices
FORCEVILLE	17.5.16		Working Parties	fly
	18.5.16		" "	fly
	19.5.16		" "	fly
	20.5.16		" "	fly
	21.5.16		Church Parade Conference 109th Brigade HQ	fly
	22.5.16		Batt took part in 109th Brigade's attack on practice trenches Fine & hot	fly
	23.5.16		" Took all 109th Brigade fatigues Fine	fly
	24.5.16		Working parties HQ spent afternoon in THIEPVAL sector Fine hot day	fly
	25.5.16		Working parties " "	fly fine day
	26.5.16		Fine two boys sent Working parties	fly
	27.5.16		" Working parties	fly
	28.5.16		Fine Church Parade Inspection of Billets & Transport lines	fly
	29.5.16		Working Parties fine & cool.	fly
	30.5.16		Still heavy rain during night Working parties	4

107th Brigade.
36th Division.

1/15th BATTALION

ROYAL IRISH RIFLES

JUNE 1916

WAR DIARY or INTELLIGENCE SUMMARY

Army Form C. 2118.

15th R. I. Rifles Vol 9

June

Place	Date	Hour	Summary of Events and Information	Remarks and references to Appendices
Forceville	31.5.16		Five Coy Officers in HAMEL trenches in afternoon. Bath in afternoon. Cooking parties.	764
MESNIL	1.6.16		Took over MESNIL from 9th R.I. Fus.	764
"	2.6.16		Brigadier came up. Afternoon Adjt & self went round R.A. O.Ps	764
"	3.6.16		Fine. 29th Div. cutting out expedition during night	764
"	4.6.16		Fine but cold	764
"	5.6.16		" " " 36th & 37th Div " " "	764
HAMEL	6.6.16		Relief sent to 10th R.I. Rifles that day. Relief completed at 1 AM	764
Trenches	7.6.16		German Artillery very active. Two men killed by T.Ms. Showers all day.	764
			Five 2/Lt Officers including Rennel & Dulgenne came round trenches. One man wounded.	764
	8.6.16		Quiet morning. At 11:30 pm violent bombardment with T.Ms, a kind of October, 5.9, 4.2; 77 mm	764
			& 8" guns. Raiding party estimated at 60 rushed WILLIAM REDAN but only 5 reached the	
	9.6.16		trench owing to rapid & machine gun fire. German ones that at close range	764
	10.6.16		but got away owing to attacking party falling over debris. 200 yds front trench	764
			absolutely flat. Communication trenches damaged. Lewis gun knocked out	764
			Casualties 9 killed 14 wounded	764
	11.6.16		Very quiet day & night	764

Army Form C. 2118.

WAR DIARY
or
INTELLIGENCE SUMMARY. 15th R. I. Rifles

(Erase heading not required.)

Instructions regarding War Diaries and Intelligence Summaries are contained in F. S. Regs., Part II. and the Staff Manual respectively. Title pages will be prepared in manuscript.

Place	Date	Hour	Summary of Events and Information	Remarks and references to Appendices
HAMEL Trenches	12.6.16		Very quiet. Brigade Conference. Capt Buchanan Sniped	July
	13.6.16		Quiet. Gun relief north 10th R. I. Rifles	July
MESNIL	14.6.16		MESNIL. Cleaning up etc	July
	15.6.16		Brigade conference	July
	16.6.16		Fire examined line from O.P.s	July
Bois d'Avely	17.6.16		AVELUY WOOD. 108 Bay conference	July
	18.6.16		Fine. Biggun assembly trenches	July
	19.6.16		Fine but dull " "	July
HAMEL	20.6.16		Relief north 16th R. I. Rifles	July
	21.6.16		Fine very quiet. Foi in Thiepval wood during enemy	July
	22.6.16		Fine morning very heavy thunderstorm. Being into 10th R. I. Rifles	July
VARENNES	23.6.16		Arrived VARENNES (last Coy) 5A.M. Fearfully wet night. Both drenched U day	July
	24.6.16		Fine V day very heavy bombardment. Practised attack dummy trenches	July
	25.6.16		Fine W " " Coy work	July
	26.6.16		Showery X " " "	July
	27.6.16		Showery Y " Marched to HEDAUVILLE	July

WAR DIARY
INTELLIGENCE SUMMARY

15th R.I. Rifles

Army Form C. 2118.

Place	Date	Hour	Summary of Events and Information	Remarks and references to Appendices
HEDAUVILLE	28.6.16		HEDAUVILLE. Attack postponed. Cold & showery	Hy
	29.6.16		½ day line. Right man slightly wounded through bomb exploding in Batt lines	Hy
	30.6.16		½ " line. Ternic Varandy. March to Thiepval at 8 p.m.	Hy

Lieut Colonel Crozier M. Whack
Comdg 15th R.I. Rifles

107th Brigade.
36th Division.

1/15th BATTALION

ROYAL IRISH RIFLES.

JULY 1916

WAR DIARY or INTELLIGENCE SUMMARY

B6/ July
Vol 10
167/36

15th R.I.R.

Place	Date	Hour	Summary of Events and Information
Thiepval	1.7.16		Arrived assembly trenches in Thiepval wood about 12.15 A.M. 583 all ranks. One man slightly wounded. Zero time 7.30 A.M. 15th in support of 108th Brigade. At 6.30 A.M. C.O. of 115th R.I. Rif asked me to closely support him owing to his heavy casualties. At 7.45 & 7.50 A.M. A & B Coys on the Right of me reported having reached German A line & estimated casualties at 60 men. C (extreme Left) & D Coys held up by enfilade machine gun fire from St. Pierre Division & being grenaded on Left by Germans who had come up out of dug outs after previous waves had passed over. Capt Chiplin (B Coy) slightly wounded. 7.55. TB line captured & C line attacked on the Right. 8.15 A.M. C & D Coys captured A line on Left. Casualties very heavy. Called for reinforcements but none available. About 10 A.M. large quantities of prisoners, maps papers etc began to come in. Communication completed, held down owing to German barrage for hours. One Coy alone sent 14 runners back only one of which got through. In the mean time on the Right C line had been captured & D line penetrated. Capt Chiplin was severely wounded ditto Capt Tate & Capt O'Flaherty killed about Hind. The machine gun enfilade fire from both flanks (the 29th & 32nd Divisions having failed) caused very heavy casualties & but by but above ground. At 8.30 P.M. Lieut Lepper returned & informed me he had only 8 N.C.Os & several of

WAR DIARY or INTELLIGENCE SUMMARY.

Army Form C. 2118.

15th R.I. Rifles

Place	Date	Hour	Summary of Events and Information	Remarks and references to Appendices
Thiepval	1.7.16		Continued of which were wounded & a lan half day men of Maced units left & that both flanks being unprotected he had had to retire. Shortly afterwards Lieut Malone went on S.I. one Rifm from further to the R came in. At 11 pm Lieut Tiptaft came in with a handful of men & informed one a message to return had reached him at 6 pm but acting on orders received from one to hold on at all cost he had done so till he found himself isolated & short of ammunition when he had retired with his entire force which now consisted of eleven men unwounded & many wounded of mixed units. During the day I sent a large quantity of bombs & S.A.A. forward but only a small quantity reached the fighting line. I also sent half of my batt bombers (the only reserves I had kept in hand) to reinforce at Allaine to a very urgent call. They were practically speaking wiped out. With the attack three lines of cable were run out but immediately broken by the bombardment Finding always to mend the wire only meant casualties & instant renewing of connection I gave up the attempt. Six newly joined officers came up to Batt HQ as reinforcements one of whom had to be sent away at once with Shell Shock	

Army Form C. 2118.

15ᵗʰ R.I.R.

WAR DIARY
or
INTELLIGENCE SUMMARY.
(Erase heading not required.)

Place	Date	Hour	Summary of Events and Information	Remarks and references to Appendices
Thiepval	2.7.16	2.6 AM	we had collected 60 O.R. onto the assembly trenches round Bath H.Q. & by 10 AM this had been increased to 120. Col Bowen informed me at 11 AM that he had information that 40 men of the 49ᵗʰ Div who had reinforced us overnight were cut off in A line & that he had instructions to reinforce with every available man of the 107ᵗʰ Brigade. I placed 100 men with four officers under the command of my batt bombing officer Lt Hogg at his disposal & at 2 pm they went over the parapet. The 15ᵗʰ being the last out of the wood suffered heavily but 25 to 30 men & all the officers (Lieuts Hogg & 2ⁿᵈ Lieut O'Connor exempted) reached the line & held it till relieved at 8 A.M. the next morning. The Batt was in recovery action for 48½ hours. At 11pm I removed my H.Q. by instructions to MARTINSART. Total Casualties 318. of which 15 were officers	Ily.
MARTINSART	3.7.16		Village shelled slightly in afternoon. Two officers & 10ᵗʰ R.I. Rifles Relief & on wounds	Ily.
"	4.7.16		marched to HARPONVILLE	Ily.
HARPONVILLE	5.7.16		Div Gen'l's parade. Marched to RUBEMPRÉ	Ily.
RUBEMPRÉ	6.7.16		Stood to 50 men at 4.5 mins notice	Ily.

Army Form C. 2118.

WAR DIARY
or
INTELLIGENCE SUMMARY.   15th R. I. Rifles

(Erase heading not required.)

Instructions regarding War Diaries and Intelligence Summaries are contained in F. S. Regs., Part II. and the Staff Manual respectively. Title pages will be prepared in manuscript.

Place	Date	Hour	Summary of Events and Information	Remarks and references to Appendices
Rubempré	7.7.16		Remained standing to at 45 min notice	7/4,
"	8.7.16		" " " 2 hours "	7/4,
"	9.7.16		" " " " "	7/4,
Bernaville	10.7.16		Marched to BERNAVILLE	7/4,
"	11.7.16		Entrained to WARDRECQUES	7/4,
Wardrecques	12.7.16		WARDRECQUES	7/4,
Bayenghem	13.7.16		Marched to BAYENGHEM.	7/4,
"	14.7.16		" " "	7/4,
"	15.7.16		" " "	7/4,
"	16.7.16		" " "	7/4,
"	17.7.16		" " "	7/4,
"	18.7.16		General Plumer met O.C. at Boujaca	7/4,
"	19.7.16		Inspection of Transport by O.C. 36th Division	7/4,
Bollezeele	20.7.16		Marched to Bollezeele	7/4,
Wormhout	21.7.16		" " Wormhout	7/4,
Hondeghem	22.7.16		" " Hondeghem	7/4,

WAR DIARY or INTELLIGENCE SUMMARY.

Army Form C. 2118.

13th R.I. Rifles.

Place	Date	Hour	Summary of Events and Information	Remarks and references to Appendices
Steenwerck	23.7.16		Marched to Steenwerck	714
"	24.7.16		"	714
"	25.7.16		"	714
"	26.7.16		"	714
"	27.7.16		"	714
"	28.7.16		"	714
Red Lodge	29.7.16		Marched to RED LODGE	714
"	30.7.16		Gas drill etc	714
"	31.7.16		Visited trenches with Brigadiers of 108th & 107th Brigades	714
			Relieve 11th R.I. Rifles in Centre Left Sector	

Letter Report to M. Clemel
Army 15th Division
Offrs

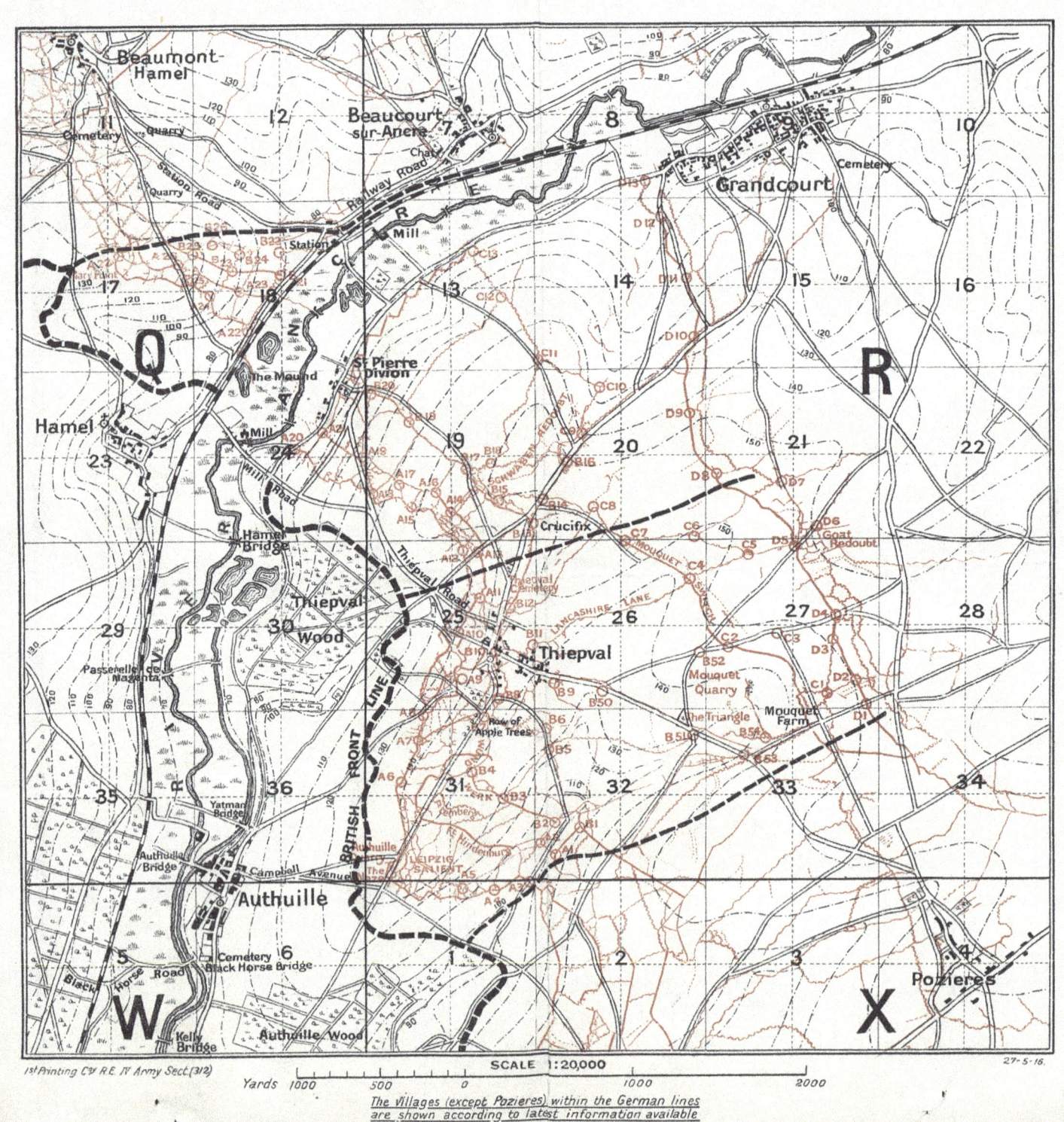

W095 2₅03
Fragmented transparent map
Section 2 of 3

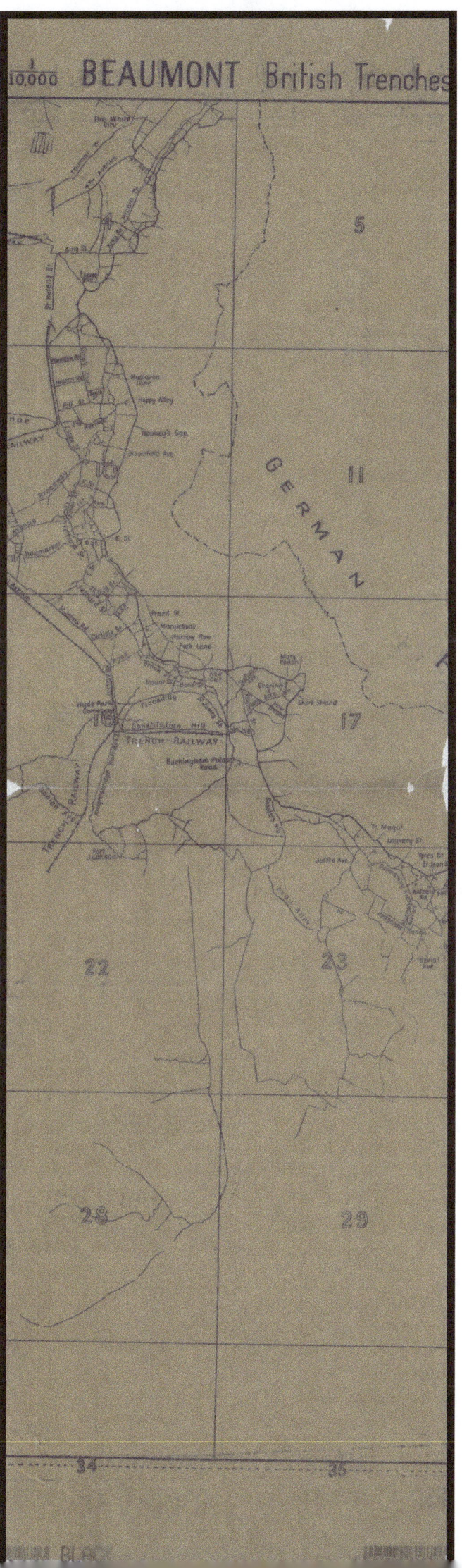

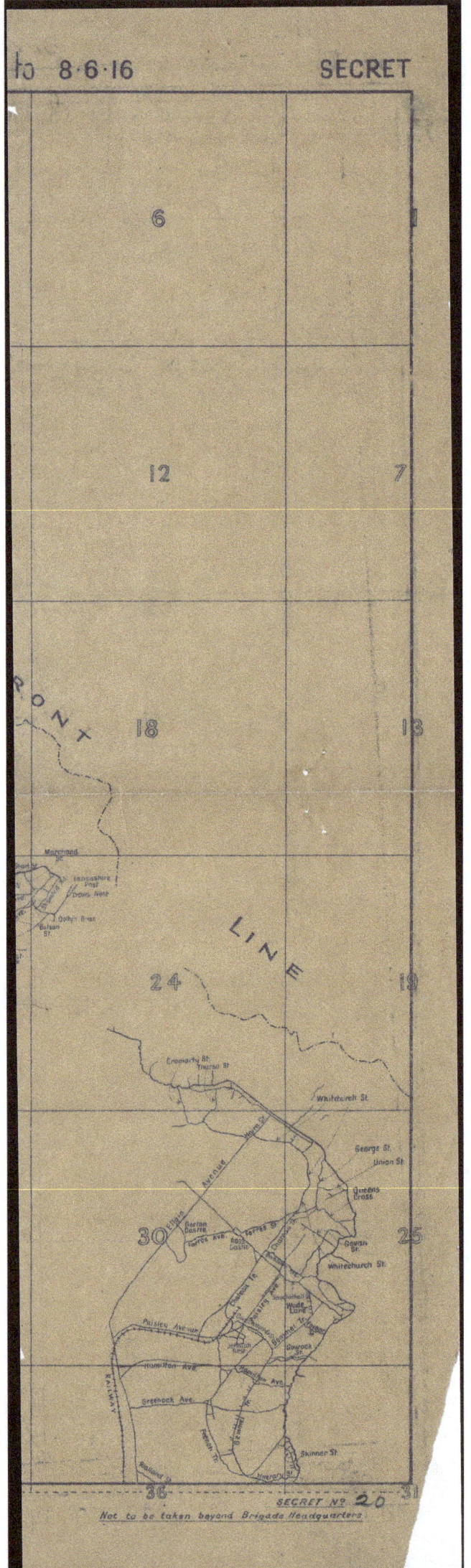

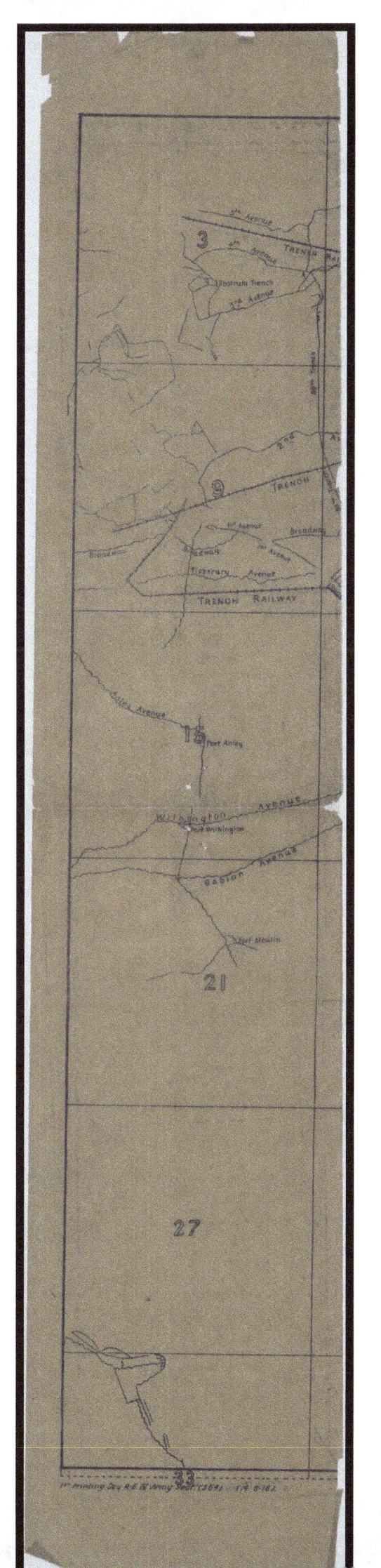

Aug-Dec
1916

Army Form C. 2118.

WAR DIARY
or
INTELLIGENCE SUMMARY. 15th R. I. Rifles

(Erase heading not required.)

Instructions regarding War Diaries and Intelligence Summaries are contained in F. S. Regs., Part II. and the Staff Manual respectively. Title pages will be prepared in manuscript.

Vol II

Place	Date	Hour	Summary of Events and Information	Remarks and references to Appendices
Trenches	1.8.16		Quiet day. G.O.C. & Brigadier came up.	
"	2.8.16		" morning. Went round with Brigadier. Fairly heavily shelled on L during afternoon	
"	3.8.16		Quiet morning. Some shelling afternoon. Machine guns quieter during night	
"	4.8.16		" " " " " 14th	
"	5.8.16		Artillery duel afternoon. Usual target. Relief with 11th R. I. Rif	1 Relief
Kortepyp	6.8.16		" "	
"	7.8.16		Quiet day.	
"	8.8.16		" " Relieved 8th R. I. Rifles in new Sector	
Trenches	9.8.16		Quiet morning. Heavy T.M. bombardment afternoon. No casualties. Heavies replied	
"	10.8.16		" " " " Two men wounded & Capt Miller	
"			Saved by S.G. but went out. Return of draft of 6 Officers & died to go to 16th.	
"	11.8.16		Usual afternoon activity	
"	12.8.16		Two fells TM bombarded at 4 p.m & 6 p.m. Exceptionally quiet night	
"	13.8.16		Usual bombardment at 5 p.m. As suggested heavies concentrated on small sector of enemy trenches doing great damage & silencing their T.M's. Night quiet	
"	14.8.16		Very quiet day & night	

Army Form C. 2118.

WAR DIARY
or
INTELLIGENCE SUMMARY.
(Erase heading not required.)

1st R. I. Rifles.

Instructions regarding War Diaries and Intelligence Summaries are contained in F. S. Regs., Part II. and the Staff Manual respectively. Title pages will be prepared in manuscript.

Place	Date	Hour	Summary of Events and Information	Remarks and references to Appendices
Trenches	15.8.16		19th Siege Battd Staff at 3.30pm. Casualties 9.7 thou mortar battery 1 officer & men killed & one man killed & three wounded	
"	16.8.16		Lylow Farm	
Lylow Farm	16.8.16		"	
"	17.8.16		Inspected 1st line Transport	
"	18.8.16		Rain. Went to Monte Noire to stay two nights. Bath & hunt to gun	
"	19.8.16		" " "	
"	20.8.16		Returned from Monte Noire. Inspected transport	
"	21.8.16		Lylow Farm. Tu Tall HQ remark etc into wrapping smoking place hatstalls	
"	22.8.16		" " "	
"	23.8.16		" NEUVE EGLISE - MESSINES road shelled during morning	
"	24.8.16		" & Bnt HQ " "	
Trenches	25.8.16		Very quiet day & night	
"	26.8.16		" " Our guns were cutting	
"	27.8.16		" " Our guns did a good deal of shooting	
"	28.8.16		Shock of a mine some way away shortly after 8 AM. Enemy fired two rounds gunfire or rounds close to HQ. One man wounded.	

Army Form C. 2118.

WAR DIARY
or
INTELLIGENCE SUMMARY.

15th R. 1 Dublins

(Erase heading not required.)

Instructions regarding War Diaries and Intelligence Summaries are contained in F. S. Regs., Part II and the Staff Manual respectively. Title pages will be prepared in manuscript.

Place	Date	Hour	Summary of Events and Information	Remarks and references to Appendices
Trenches	29.8.16.		Very wet day but Quiet. Conference at 10th Battn H.Q. last night	
"	30.8.16		Trenches full of water. Full strong S.W. wind. Heavy rain. Quiet day. Artillery strafe at 1.30 A.M. Germans put very little back	Ily.
"	31.8.16		Fine morning. Brigadier came up	Ily.

Army Form C. 2118.

WAR DIARY 15th Bn R. Irish Rifles

INTELLIGENCE SUMMARY.

(Erase heading not required.)

Instructions regarding War Diaries and Intelligence Summaries are contained in F.S. Regs., Part II and the Staff Manual respectively. Title pages will be prepared in manuscript.

Vol 12

Place	Date	Hour	Summary of Events and Information	Remarks and references to Appendices
In the field	1.9.16		Gas liberated by Bde. on our immediate right	R
Kortepyp	2.9."		Divisional Reserve. Battalion arms equipment &c inspected. Wet day	R
do	3 "		do Wet day Lecture to NCOs by Regt. Sergt Major	R
do	4th "		do Lecture by Prof. Atkin at Bailleul subject The Balkans	R
do	5 "		do	R
do	6th "		do Gas alarm	R
do	7 "		do	R
do	8 "		do Gas alarm	R
do	9 "		do Relieved 8th Bn. R.I.R. in Trenches	R
In the field	10 "		Trenches Very quiet day & night - Inspected by Brigadier	R
do	11 "		do Conference re Bde. Defence Scheme	R
do	12 "		do Lt McQuiston ordered to England	R
do	13 "		do Wet afternoon - Inspection of trenches by Divisional Sanitary Officer	R
do	14 "		do Quiet day & night. Fine but cold	R
do	15 "		do Raid carried out by 9th Bn R.I.R. 1 prisoner captured. quiet day & night	R
do	16 "		do Bombardment 10am to 12 noon & 3pm to 5pm. Quiet on our front	R

Army Form C. 2118.

WAR DIARY
INTELLIGENCE SUMMARY.   15th Bn. R. Irish Rifles
(Erase heading not required.)

Place	Date	Hour	Summary of Events and Information	Remarks and references to Appendices
In the field	17.9.16		Trenches. Enemy shelled our trenches during morning 5 men wounded by shrapnel apparently in retaliation for our artillery opening on one of their working parties killing one man. Relief by 8th Bn R.I.R.	R
Neuve Eglise	18.9."		Bde. Reserve H.Q. at NEUVE EGLISE. C/Sgt. killed in tram weather wet	R
"	19.9."		do. B Coy moved to ZYLO FARM weather very wet. working parties	R
"	20.9."		do. working parties	R
"	21.9."		do. Visited Transport - Fine. Patrol sent to examine locality for proposed raid	R
"	22.9."		do. Spitlocke) trees of German trench - Fine	R
"	23.9."		do. Practised raiding party on trees as above. Brigadier present. Relief by 8th Bn R.I.R.	R
In the Field	24.9."		Trenches. Enemy machine gun emplacement opposite Dragond bombarded. Lecture at Bailleul	R
"	25.9."		do. Quiet day - weather fine	R
"	26.9."		do. Enemy observed strengthening their parapet with concrete blocks	R
"	27.9."		do. About 6 p.m hostile observation balloon brought down in flames behind the line	R
"	28.9."		do. Bombardment by our trench mortars of enemy's 2nd line - Retaliation slight	R
"	29.9."		do. Relieved by 8th Bn R.I.R. weather showery H.Q. to Kortepyp	R
Kortepyp	30.9."		Divisional Reserve Inspected Battn. paraded as strong as possible in fighting order & afterwards in fatigue dress	R

Rooke Major Commdg 15th R.I.R.

Army Form C. 2118.

WAR DIARY
or
INTELLIGENCE SUMMARY.

15th R. I. Rifles

(Erase heading not required.)

Instructions regarding War Diaries and Intelligence Summaries are contained in F. S. Regs., Part II. and the Staff Manual respectively. Title pages will be prepared in manuscript.

Vol. 19

Place	Date	Hour	Summary of Events and Information	Remarks and references to Appendices
KORTEPYP	Oct 1st		Fine day. Dry work	Francis Sproule Lt Col. 15th R.I.Rifles
"	" 2nd		" " "	
"	" 3rd		Wet morning	
"	" 4th		" day	
"	" 5th		Relief with 8th R.I. Rifles	
Trenches	" 6th		Fine. Semi very dirty & not quiet	
"	" 7th		Wet. Very quiet day.	
"	" 8th		Wet morning, the rest gas at 1.30.AM from L Bat sector. German retaliation very much [One man wounded
"	" 9th		Fine. Very quiet morning. T.M. shells on L 2.30 to 3.30 pm. Fairly quiet night
"	" 10th		Lovely morning. Some shelling. Fired L.G. in Surrey LANE. Intense sniping at 3AM. One Sapper killed
"	" 11th		Relief with 8th R.I.R. Heavy T.M. bombardment during afternoon & early evening
Neuve Eglise	" 12th		Neuve Eglise	
"	" 13th		"	
"	" 14th		"	
"	" 15th		"	
"	" 16th		" General inspected Transport lines	

WAR DIARY or INTELLIGENCE SUMMARY

Army Form C. 2118.

15th R.I. Rifles

Place	Date	Hour	Summary of Events and Information	Remarks and references to Appendices
Neuve Eglise	Oct 17th		Relief with 8th R.I. Rifles	
Trenches	" 18th		Trenches very wet. All Cy HAs in front line have been knocked in. Great day & night	*see Appendix. to W.D. 15 R.I.R*
"	" 19th		Very wet day. Knocking very active at night. Two officers went out to examine wire for raiding purposes	
"	" 20th		Fine day. All dug-outs in front line flooded. 14"g water in cellar in trop Medumi H.A.T. & Supply line falling	
"	" 20th		in also all bays in Er Brigadier Brig Major & 6th TM officer came up to view cutting	
"	" 21st		Very cold night. Quiet. Lovely day. Germans came to look place of entry for raid. One casualty	
"	" 22nd		Bitter cold night. Lovely day. Very quiet	
"	" 23rd		Fine, not so cold. Relief with 8th R.I. Rifles	
"	" 24th		KORTEPYP. Gottschue Trenches to practice raid. Wet day	
"	" 25th		" Practised " " " Wet day	
"	" 26th		" " " " " " "	
"	" 27th		" " " " " " Brigadier & Brigade saw us at practice	
"	" 28th		" Brigadier inspected Transport. Night practice over spotted ground using very lights	
"	" 29th		" Showery. Relief with 8th R.I.R.	
"	" 30th		Quiet day. Raid party went out 2.40 A.M. One party of only 8 bolts & had to be forced & opened by 2nd Lieut Clark. German trench entered at 4.30. Sentry killed. Germans meeting to our	

WAR DIARY or INTELLIGENCE SUMMARY

Army Form C. 2118.

15th R. I. Rifles

Place	Date	Hour	Summary of Events and Information	Remarks and references to Appendices
Trenches	0130	continued	Opened a very heavy fire of hand grenades from the front & both flanking bays of the bay we had entered. Forced to retire. Casualties Lt Bolton & 7 men wounded & two men missing one known to be killed. Previous to entry in their trench the German wire had been surprisingly quiet owing very probably to the very light. This being the only place where the wire was cut it is believed they laid up for us.	Issue Henry 1st 15 R.I. Rifles
"	6.0 am		Showery with bright sunny spells. Brigadier came up & later inspected & then German shelter back of front line of the R.I.Rif in the morning	

Army Form C. 2118.

WAR DIARY
OR
INTELLIGENCE SUMMARY. 1st R.I. Rifles
(Erase heading not required.)

Vol 14

Louis Morten Lieut

Place	Date	Hour	Summary of Events and Information	Remarks and references to Appendices
Trenches	1.11.16		Fine. Quiet. R.F.C. very active	
"	2.11.16		Wet night & morning. Fine afternoon. Very quiet. two casualties.	
"	3 "		Fine day. French motor bombardment.	
"	4 "		Fine. Holiday.	
Neuve Eglise	5 "		Wet day	
"	6.11.16		" Inspected Transport	
"	7.11.16		Showery	
"	8.11.16		"	
"	9.11.16		Wet day	
"	10.11.16		Fine. Relieved 8th R.I. Rifles. Relieving quiet	
Trenches	11.11.16		Trenches in very bad state. All huts along river washed away into latrine in Barbary Coast. Left C Co in very bad state. Berry Lane bad. King Edward II impassable. Loop only approachable from Dugout which is deep in water. 3" water in Coy H.Q. 14" in Cellar. Brigadier & R.E. Officer came up to drainage. Very quiet	
"	12.11.16		Fine quiet day	
"	13.11.16		Very fine. Quiet	

Army Form C. 2118.

WAR DIARY
or
INTELLIGENCE SUMMARY. 1st R. I. Rifles

(Erase heading not required.)

Place	Date	Hour	Summary of Events and Information	Remarks and references to Appendices
Trenches	14.11.16.		Very fine. Surrey Lane Shelter. One man killed. Quiet night	Issue Nights Kit out
"	15.11.16		" " Heavy T.M. bombardment backed by two R.A. from 11.30 A.M. to 12 P.M.	
"	16.11.16		Fine. Relief with 8th R.I. Rifles	
Kortepyp	17.11.16		Hard frost	
"	18.11.16		Hard frost during night. Turned to rain during day	
"	19.11.16		Still a thaw. New draft 76 O.R. arrived	
"	20.11.16		Inspected draft. Took it through drill. Stole last time	
"	21.11.16		Brigadier inspected draft. Fine but dull	
"	22.11.16		G.O.C. inspected new draft. Brigadier inspected camp. Relieved 8th Batt	
Trenches	23.11.16		Fine. Quiet day	
"	24.11.16		Quiet.	
"	25.11.16		Rained most of the day. Quiet	
"	26.11.16		Fine. We blew up enemy wire with an aerial torpedo at 8 p.m. No retaliation on right front	
"	27.11.16		08.4 A.M. enemy stupidly bombed his own wire & Grand M.G. fire. Two casualties on working party	
			Fine. Quiet. Enemy again bombed his own wire during night	
"	28.11.16		Fine heavy fog. G.O.C. came round C.s. Did a lot of wiring in front of C1. Relief day	

Army Form C. 2118.

WAR DIARY
or
INTELLIGENCE SUMMARY.

15th R.I. Rifles

(Erase heading not required.)

Place	Date	Hour	Summary of Events and Information	Remarks and references to Appendices
Neuve Eglise	29.11.16		Very cold & foggy. Inspected new draft	7th
"	30.11.16		" " " " Changed Batt. H.Q. Venture 36 Bri. School	7th

Army Form C. 2118.

15th R.I. Rifles

Vol 15

WAR DIARY
or
INTELLIGENCE SUMMARY.
(Erase heading not required.)

Place	Date	Hour	Summary of Events and Information	Remarks and references to Appendices
Mum Eglise	1/12/16		Bitterly cold. Gas alarm at 11pm, also at 1am.	Letter B issued by
	2/12/16		Bitterly cold day. Firing went working parties	
	3/12/16		Bitterly cold day.	
	4/12/16		Fine. Relieved the 8th R.I. Rifles at 4-30 pm. Rain hard day & night	
Trenches	5/12/16		Fine. Much trench artillery very active.	
	6/12/16		Dull day. T.M. Bombardment 7.50 am to 7.25 am.	
	7/12/16		Fine day. unusually quiet.	
	8/12/16		Enemy artillery active in the morning. No damage done	
	9/12/16		Enemy artillery very active about 11 am, very little damage. Wet afternoon	
	10/12/16		Corps Commander visited the Bricks Marsion, two cases of Scarlet fever. 8th R.I. Rifles relieved us at 4-30pm	
Inkerman Huts	11/12/16		'B' Company isolated because of isolated men. Usual parades.	
	12/12/16		A.D.M.S. inspected the isolated men. Usual parades.	
	13/12/16		Usual parades, weather wet. Four cases of suspected scarlet fever returned.	
	14/12/16		Very wet morning, usual parades in afternoon.	
	15/12/16		Weather wet. usual parades in the morning.	
Trenches	16/12/16		Relieved the 8th R.I. Rifles at 4-55 pm. Very quiet night to rain.	

Army Form C. 2118.

15th R.I. Rifles

WAR DIARY
or
INTELLIGENCE SUMMARY.
(Erase heading not required.)

Instructions regarding War Diaries and Intelligence Summaries are contained in F.S. Regs. Part II. and the Staff Manual respectively. Title pages will be prepared in manuscript.

Place	Date	Hour	Summary of Events and Information	Remarks and references to Appendices
Banvillers	17/12/16		Enemy artillery very active 3.30pm, Shelled C2 for 30½ minutes, our Retaliation very bad, Short of ammunition.	Letter B. Event Ays
	18/12/16		" " " " No damage. Quiet night. No rain.	
	19/12/16		Active at 3pm	
	20/12/16		Very active at 3pm. Fired 30 Rounds 5.9's on Mt Auson Rd, 1 Killed 3 wounded on the Road	
	21/12/16		Very quiet all day. No rain.	
	22/12/16		Relieved by 8th R.I. Rifles 4 pm	
Mean Felix	23/12/16		Usual inspection, Battalion turned up, the Isolettes juried very clear. this day	
	24/12/16		Working parties as usual. Fine day	
	25/12/16		Very wet early in the morning. Enemy artillery fired 300 Rounds of 5.9.3 on to Jomden & Shellitti Hub	
	26/12/16		Usual working parties, any artillery active on the Dam places as the 26th	
	27/12/16		Usual working parties. Fine day.	
	28/12/16		Relieved the 8th R.I. Rifles at 4-10 p.m. very heavy rain very FC night.	
Banvillers B	29/12/16		Took over New line from the 108th Brigade, Trenches very bad owing to previous nights rain.	
	30/12/16		Very quiet day. No rain. Unusually quiet night.	
	31/12/16		Enemy artillery active all day and also at 11pm at night no damage weather fine.	

Jon-Dee

1917

Army Form C. 2118.

WAR DIARY
or
INTELLIGENCE SUMMARY.   15ᵗʰ R 1. Rifles
(Erase heading not required.)

Instructions regarding War Diaries and Intelligence Summaries are contained in F. S. Regs., Part II. and the Staff Manual respectively. Title pages will be prepared in manuscript.

Place	Date	Hour	Summary of Events and Information	Remarks and references to Appendices
Trenches	1.1.17		A fair amount of shelling all day. Fine	Name History 15.1.17 9.1. Rifles
"	2.1.17		Enemy artillery active during afternoon. Quiet night. Some rain	
"	3.1.17		" Morning. Casualties 1 killed one wounded. Relief ?	
Kortepyp	4.1.17		Very wet morning. Usual inspections	
"	5 " "		Usual working parties	
"	6 " "		Very cold	
"	7 " "		" Showers all day	
"	8 " "		" & wet	
"	9 " "		Fine. Relieved 8ᵗʰ R.I. Rifles in trenches	
Trenches	10 " "		Brigadier came up. R by trench state. Some shelling. One killed one wounded	
"	11 " "		" " Quiet morning. Snow	
"	12 " "		Snowing & cold. Enemy active during afternoon	
"	13 " "		Bitterly cold. Enemy artillery very active	
"	14 " "		" " Very quiet	
"	15 " "		" " " Relief night	
Neuve Eglise	16 " "			

Army Form C. 2118.

WAR DIARY
or
INTELLIGENCE SUMMARY.
(Erase heading not required.)

15th R. I. Rifles

Vol 16

Place	Date	Hour	Summary of Events and Information	Remarks and references to Appendices
Neuve Eglise	17 Jan		Usual working parties. Snow	
"	18 "		Two Coys in huts relieved reserve Coys in trenches. Snow	
"	19 "		Very cold	
"	20 "		Very cold. C.O. returned from commanding Officers 1st Army conference	
"	21 "		" " Inspected transport. Relief. Quiet night	
Trenches	22 "		Quiet morning. Very intense bombardment from 3pm to 7pm on Reg 109 Bgd & 25th Bde	Lieut Gordon left Depot
"	23 "		Very cold. Quiet morning. 107 & 109 Brigadiers came round	
"	24 "		Enemy artillery very active. Several direct hits but line of communication ok. Very cold	
"	25 "		Very cold. Enemy artillery very active on back area round guns. 1 gun from 108 Brig came up	
"	26 "		Frost harder than ever. Quiet day	
"	27 "		Very hard frost. Bright & sunny. Relief with 11th R.I. Rifles	15th
Aldershot	28 "		Intense cold	
"	29 "		" " Visited work all officers. Reference to Hill 63	
"	30 "		" " Snow in afternoon	
"	31 "		Not quite so " Snow showers	

2353 Wt. W2544/1454 700,000 5/15 D. D. & L. A.D.S.S. Forms/C 2118.

WAR DIARY
or
INTELLIGENCE SUMMARY.
(Erase heading not required.)

Army Form C. 2118.

15th R.I. Rifles

Place	Date	Hour	Summary of Events and Information	Remarks and references to Appendices
ALDERSHOT	Feb 1st		Very hard frost. G.O.C. came up. Conference at Brigade afternoon	
"	2nd		" " " "	
"	3rd		" " " " All Officers visited KEMIL defences	
"	4th		" " " " Usual Training	
"	5th		" " " " "	
"	6th		" " " " "	
"	7th		" " " " " Two drafts arrived 59 & 183 O.R.	
"	8th		" " " " " Brigadier inspected drafts	
"	9th		" " " " "	
"	10th		" " " " Marched to METERIN	
METERIN	11th		Snow started Platoon Training Bayonet Competition	
"	12th		" " " "	
"	13th		" " very heavy Coy " "	
"	14th		" " " " Coy " Brigadier inspected musketry	
"	15th		" " " " Coy Schemes	
"	16th		" " rapid " "	

2353 Wt. W2544/1454 700,000 5/15 D. D. & L. A.D.S.S. Forms/C. 2118.

Army Form C. 2118.

WAR DIARY
or
INTELLIGENCE SUMMARY.   15th R.1. Rifles
(Erase heading not required.)

Place	Date	Hour	Summary of Events and Information	Remarks and references to Appendices
METERIN	Feb 17th		Thaw very rapid	Major Morton 16 & 15th R.I. Rif.
"	18th		Heavy Mist. Batt scheme	
	19th		Rain all day. Route march money	
	20th		Thick fog. Bath bill	
	21st		" " Half Batt bathing remainder by Coys	
	22nd		Rain " "	
	23rd		Thick fog. Bath Scheme	
	24th		Fine dull. Route march	
	25th		Cleaning up preparing to move	
	26th		Took over billets in R Scherts Reserve. draft 17 O.R. arrived	
	27th		Went round front line with Brigadier	
	28th		Inspected front line. Visited ADMS. Gas were afternoon	
March	1st		G.O.C. Came up also Brigadier	

WAR DIARY
or
INTELLIGENCE SUMMARY.

(Erase heading not required.)

Army Form C. 2118.

15th R. I. Rifles

Vol 18

Place	Date	Hour	Summary of Events and Information	Remarks and references to Appendices
Catacombes	2/3/17		Interview with G.O.C. 2nd Army. Usual working parties	
"	March 3rd		Relief with 8th R.I. Rifles	
Trenches	"	4th	Very quiet morning. Just O.C. Batt on our left (Anzacs) went round subsidiary lines & posts	
"	"	5th	R.A. active during afternoon. Snow. Very quiet	
"	"	6th	Fine. Brigadier Wethersole came up to say goodbye to the month	
"	"	7th	Fine. We bombarded MESINES heavily at 11 A.M. Very quiet on our own front	
"	"	8th	Fine. Enemy very active on Wychaete front making several raids during the night. Our guns firing according to plan from 7pm to 5am. Hand to hand	
"	"	9th	Enemy put over a few shells onto our front & support line. Snow. Relieving.	
Catacombes	"	10th	Fine. Coy officers away inspecting new line Nrg Wulverghem - Wytschaete Rd.	
"	"	11th	Conference at Brigade	
"	"	12th	Marched to Derry Hts & Kemmel Roon	
Trenches	"	13th	Took over Spanbroek Sector from 1st Munsters.	
"	"	14th	Fine very quiet day	
"	"	15th	" " " A sniper killed one man & struck a civilian	

Army Form C. 2118.

WAR DIARY
or
INTELLIGENCE SUMMARY.
(Erase heading not required.)

1st R. I. Rifles

Instructions regarding War Diaries and Intelligence Summaries are contained in F.S. Regs., Part II. and the Staff Manual respectively. Title pages will be prepared in manuscript.

Place	Date	Hour	Summary of Events and Information	Remarks and references to Appendices
Trenches	March 16th		Very quiet day. Went round with Brigadier. Patrols out from 10pm	
"	" 17th		Corpsman with Brigadier & G.O.C. Our R.A. relieved 16th Div	
"	" 18th		Still morning. Vyoni later in quiet	
"	" 19th		Enemy firing very active in back area this morning. Heavy rain afternoon. Enemy put 40 TMs over & cut the wire we had put out. Raid anticipated. Coys stood to til relief	
Kemmel	" 20th		Trenches. Enemy put a few shells into village.	
"	" 21st		Kemmel shelled during night & at 2 AM. Some casualties to 108th MG & TM men	
"	" 22nd		" again. DF SM Brown slightly wounded	
"	" 23rd		Kemmel again shelled	
"	" 24th		Very heavy enemy bombardment at 4 AM. Stood To at 4.30 AM. & Down at 6.25 AM	
"	" 25th		Relief day. Quiet. Summer time started at 11PM	
Trenches	" 26th		Fine. Quiet morning. Snow showers. Enemy very active with TMs & 77MMs afternoon	
"	" 27th		Snow showers. A few shells put into Piccadilly during morning	
"	" 28th		Fine. Our TMs & 18 pdrs cut wire	
"	" 29th		Heavy rain. Very quiet day	
"	" 30th		Showery. Very quiet morning. Enemy TMs active afternoon	
"	" 31st		Showery. Light artillery & T.M. activity. Relief costs ?	

Signed Edgerton Lt Col
O/C 1st R.I. Rifles

R.I. Rifles

Army Form C. 2118.

WAR DIARY
or
INTELLIGENCE SUMMARY.

(Erase heading not required.)

15th R. Irish Rifles

Vol 19

Place	Date	Hour	Summary of Events and Information	Remarks and references to Appendices
DERRY HUTS NEAR KEMMEL	April 1st		Hail storm. Battalion in DERRY HUTS after relief from trenches	
	2nd		Cold & showery. Usual working parties.	
	3rd		Heavy snow during night, thaw at mid-day. During course of afternoon enemy in searching	
		7.0 p.m	for one of our batteries put shrapnel over the huts.	
	4th		Dull & showery. Nothing of importance.	
	5th		Fine weather. Enemy aeroplane engaged overhead & brought down by one of our machines, & turned the guard to be German 'plane, an Albatros scout, which fell very close to our trench. The pilot, Lt. Fink was wounded. During afternoon our trench shelled. Two huts were hit but only one casualty. Again at 9.0 p.m shelling was repeated, but no casualties though several huts were pierced by shrapnel.	
QUATRE -	6th		Fine. Battalion moved out of the line & split up. "A" Coy. went to 171st Coy. R.E. (Tunnelling),	
FILS AYMON			"B", "C", "D" Coys. engaged on railway work between BAILLEUL and METEREN. Battn. Hqrs. and details went to QUATRE FILS AYMON, near METEREN.	
	7th-8th		Fine. Nothing of note.	
	9th		Snow sleet. Conference of Battalion Commanders at Brigade Hqrs. G.O.C. (Maj. Gnl. O.S.W. Nugent, C.B., D.S.O.) attended.	

Army Form C. 2118.

WAR DIARY
or
INTELLIGENCE SUMMARY.
(Erase heading not required.)

Place	Date	Hour	Summary of Events and Information	Remarks and references to Appendices
QUATRE FILS AYMON	10th–14th		Changeable weather. Nothing of note.	
HAZEBROUCK	15th		Battalion commenced march to training area. Billeted at HAZEBROUCK this night.	
HALLINES	16th		March continued, 17 miles to HALLINES.	
ACQUIN	17th		Reached training area, billets at ACQUIN. Hail storm en route routed 1st Battalion.	
"	18th		Rain all day. Today spent in such desired inspection of kits.	
"	19th		Slight rain. Platoon training began.	
"	20th		Fine. Platoon training. Detachment of "A" Coy, ½ half of "C" re-joined at night.	
"	21st		" " " "	
"	22nd		" Rehearsal of Company training at BOIS DE L'EGLISE, near VAL D'ACQUIN.	
"	23rd		" Company scheme before Maj. Gen. Nugent.	
"	24th		" Battalion scheme, attack in entrenched position, near QUELMES	
"	25th		" Battalion scheme, attack on village, at CORMETTES	
"	26th		" " " " before Maj. Gen. Nugent.	
"	27th–28th		" Brigade Scheme near ZUDAUSQUES, on 27th C.Off.(L.Col. J.L. Gordon) injured.	
"	29th		V.Fine. No parades	
HALLINES	30th		V.Fine. March back toward line began, arrived at HALLINES at mid-day.	

Army Form C. 2118.

15th R.I. Rifles

Vol 20

Rouen Monday 15.7.1918

WAR DIARY
or
INTELLIGENCE SUMMARY.
(Erase heading not required.)

Instructions regarding War Diaries and Intelligence Summaries are contained in F.S. Regs., Part II. and the Staff Manual respectively. Title pages will be prepared in manuscript.

Place	Date	Hour	Summary of Events and Information	Remarks and references to Appendices
HAZEBROUCK	May 1st		March continued to Hazebrouck. Fine & hot	
PRINCBOOM	2nd		Arrived into billets at PRINCBOOM	
"	3rd		Fine & hot. Coy training	
"	4th		Very hot. B Coy & part of C left for KEERSEBROM to work on railway	
"	5th		Some rain. Remainder of B " " & half A Coy proceeded to 171 Coy RE	
"	6th		Fine " A & B0 OR from C Coy " " " "	
"	7th		Fine. 36th Div. Horse Show at DRANOUTRE. 2nd prize officers chargers & 3rd mules	
"	8th to 12th		Fine. Bns split up	
"	13th		Fine. Reinforcement 2 officers & 51 ORs draft from 1/20th LONDON Regt joined	
"	14th		Rain. Bn at his working parties moves into Bivouacs E of BAILLEUL 2 officers	
BIVOUACS	15th		Fine. Usual working parties	
"	16th		Fine " "	Scherpenberg
"	17th		Heavy rain at night. all available officers & men warned orders at "	
"	18th		Fine " "	
"	19 & 23rd		Fine Usual work. Officers visits OPs. " "	
"	24th		Evening. The night we carried out a raid in the SPANBROEK. Lots	

WAR DIARY or INTELLIGENCE SUMMARY

15th R. I. Rifles Army Form C. 2118.

Place	Date	Hour	Summary of Events and Information	Remarks and references to Appendices
BIVOUACS	May 25		The party consisted of 2nd Lieut HOGG in command, 2nd Lieut W. WHEELER & 38 ORs. That line was found empty but support line was strongly held. Enemy put down a prompt & heavy barrage. Lieut Wheeler badly wounded in both legs. Lieut Hogg badly wounded & carried to post line by Corpl BREEN & after raiding party had been withdrawn carried across NOMANS Land by Cpl Breen & Sgt STEAD but now gun Lt & Rifm Total casualties 1 Officer killed one wounded & 5 ORs wounded.	Francis Hodges Lieut 15th R I Rifles
"	26		2nd Lieut. Mr Hogg buried in POND Cemetery	
"	27		Trench Normal work	
"	28		" " "	
"	29		" " "	
"	30		" Brigade Conference	
"	31		" Marched to Triouvaux in BERTHEN area	

WAR DIARY
or
INTELLIGENCE SUMMARY.
(Erase heading not required.)

Army Form C. 2118.

15th R.I. Rifles.

Vol 21

Place	Date	Hour	Summary of Events and Information	Remarks and references to Appendices
Bertha	June 1st		Gen. Withycombe returned and took over	
"	" 2nd		Practiced attack.	
"	" 3rd		Practiced attack. Detachments abt 20 men joined up. Very hot.	
"	" 4th		Practiced attack. Inspections. Very hot.	
"	" 5th		Practiced attack.	
Trenches	" 6th		Marched to advanced area and then to Sct Trenches.	
"	" 7th		Zero hour 3-10 P.M. Mines and attack went off punctually. All objectives taken according to schedule. D.Coy. heavy casualties from Sct Trenches to No Mans Land. Capt. Hind and 2/Lt. Beaty wounded. Lt. Addy slightly wounded. Hq. moved to ENFER WOOD about 9:30 A.M. Front line continuous with Brigade on RIGHT and LEFT. An outpost line was thrown out in conjunction with barrage movements. Two machine guns, 1 field gun, complete listening set, and telephone sets, besides prisoners were captured. At 5-0 P.M. the 12th R.I. RIFLES and troops of the 11th Div. passed through attacking and capturing the OOSSTAVERNE. We were relieved at 1-30 A.M. going back to BEE HIVE dugouts for the night. Casualties 12 O.Rs killed, 5 officers, 86 O.Rs wounded. 2/Lt. Gilmore and 2/Lt. Morrison slightly wounded.	

WAR DIARY or INTELLIGENCE SUMMARY

1st R. I. Rifles Army Form C. 2118.

Place	Date	Hour	Summary of Events and Information	Remarks and references to Appendices
Trenches	June 8th		Batt. re-equipping. 6.30 P.M. heavy counter attack on Messines. All quiet at 9.20 P.M.	
Dranoutre	" 9th		Marched to DRANOUTRE.	
	" 10th		Batt. parade.	
	" 11th		Batt. parade.	
	" 12th		Brigade parade.	
	" 13th		Marched to CROIX DE POPERINGE area.	
Croix de Poperinghe	" 14th		Batt. parade.	
	" 15th		Very hot.	
	" 16th		Very hot.	
	" 17th		Orders to reconnoitre LUMM FARM and Line EAST.	
Trenches	" 18th		Marched to KEMMEL. Capt. Miller and 2/Lts. Stirling and Evans.	
	" 19th		Trenches. 1 man killed, 2 men wounded on relief at L'ENVER WOOD.	
	" 20th		Bosch shelled all day, and one of his planes brought down two of our Sausages.	
	" 21st		Fine but much cooler. Bosch artillery active. Meeting of 36th Div. and 25th Div. at 15th R.I. Rifles	
	" 22nd		IX Corps rest station re. LUMM FARM.	
			Enemy artillery active. Capt. Coulson evacuated, sick.	

15th R.I. Regt.

Army Form C. 2118.

WAR DIARY
or
INTELLIGENCE SUMMARY.
(Erase heading not required.)

Instructions regarding War Diaries and Intelligence Summaries are contained in F.S. Regs., Part II. and the Staff Manual respectively. Title pages will be prepared in manuscript.

Place	Date	Hour	Summary of Events and Information	Remarks and references to Appendices
Trenches	June 23rd		Capt. Potter proceeded on leave.	See Appx 15/1/28 etc.
"	" 24th		Lt. Col. Gordon evacuated, sick. Relieved 8th Battn. R.I. Rifles in Right Brigade Sub-sector.	
"	" 25th		(FRONT LINE). 4 men slightly wounded in relief at CABIN HILL.	
"	" 26th		Enemy artillery active day and night. Day fair.	
"	" 27th		Enemy artillery active day and night. Day fine. 1 man wounded.	
"	" 28th		Enemy artillery quiet. Day fine. 1 casualty.	
"	" 28th		Enemy artillery moderately quiet. Heavy thunderstorms during which Battn. was relieved by 10th Battn. R. Fus.	See Appx
Clare Camp	" 29th		Arrived in CLARE CAMP at 4-30 A.M.	
Outtersteene	" 30th		Marched to Billets in MERRIS AREA.	

Army Form C. 2118.

WAR DIARY
or
INTELLIGENCE SUMMARY.
(Erase heading not required.)

15 R Bulls R.J.
Vol 2

Instructions regarding War Diaries and Intelligence Summaries are contained in F. S. Regs., Part II. and the Staff Manual respectively. Title pages will be prepared in manuscript.

Place	Date	Hour	Summary of Events and Information	Remarks and references to Appendices
MERRIS AREA	1.7.17		Lt. Col. F.L. Gordon D.S.O.	
"	2.7.17		Renewed Batt. Bailleul Bombed. 1 Horse, 1 Mule, 1 Groom Wounded.	
"	3.7.17		Fine & cool. Coys work. Lieut J.F. Stewart came as Adjutant.	
"	4.7.17		Very hot. Brigade Route March	
"	5.7.17		" Coy work	
"	6.7.17		Started march 7.0.a.m for CAESTRE AREA	
"	7.7.17		" " 4.30.a.m " RENNESCURE "	
"	8.7.17		" " 3.45.a.m " ACQUIN.	
ACQUIN AREA	9.7.17		Church-morning. Coys training - Afternoon.	
"	10.7.17		Thunder training - morning.	
"	11.7.17		" - Afternoon A.T. Area.	
"	12.7.17		" morning A.3. "	
"	13.7.17		Fine training morning Bt. Area.	
"	14.7.17		Holiday	
"	15.7.17		Thunder Showers training - afternoon.	
"	16.7.17		Very close " - morning	
"			" " Night Operation	

Army Form C. 2118.

WAR DIARY
or
INTELLIGENCE SUMMARY.
(Erase heading not required.)

Instructions regarding War Diaries and Intelligence Summaries are contained in F. S. Regs., Part II. and the Staff Manual respectively. Title pages will be prepared in manuscript.

Place	Date	Hour	Summary of Events and Information	Remarks and references to Appendices
ACQUIN AREA	17.7.17		Training – two hours morning.	
"	18.7.17		Very wet day. Sports postponed.	
"	19.7.17		Fine. Batt. Relieved.	
"	20.7.17		" "	
"	21.7.17		" "	
"	22.7.17		Brigade Rifle Scheme. Bn. Sports.	
"	23.7.17		Fine. Batt. at "A" Range.	
"	24.7.17		" Brigade Scheme. G.O.C. present. M.19ᵈ	
"	25.7.17		Wet morning – fine afternoon. Bus to WINNEZEELE.	
WINNEZEELE	26.7.17 to 28.7.17		Rested at WINNEZEELE.	
"	29.7.17		Moved to the WATOU AREA.	
"	30.7.17			
WATOU AREA	31.7.17		Heavy rain. Rested WATOU AREA.	

W. Montgomery Major.
Comdg. 3rd Bn. Royal I. Rifles.

A6945 Wt. W14422/M160 350,000 12/16 D. D. & L. Forms/C/2118/14

WAR DIARY or INTELLIGENCE SUMMARY

Army Form C. 2118.

15-R.I.R. Vol 23

Place	Date	Hour	Summary of Events and Information	Remarks and references to Appendices
	1917 August			
WATOU	1	—	Short day here. Very wet.	
"	2	4 a.m.	Moved to YPRES. occupied CONGREVE WALK & BIRCH LANE trenches during day.	
"	"	9.45 p.m.	Relieved three battalions of 55th Div. in BLACK LINE through enemy barrage.	
"	"	—	Pouring rain & ground 18" deep in mud.	
YPRES	3	—	Battalions in BLACK LINE. Heavy shelling at 9.45 a.m. Still wet.	
"	4	—	Still in BLACK LINE. Enemy guns active. Weather dry.	
"	5	—	Still in BLACK LINE. Relieved by 8th Bn. R. So. Rifles & moved into BLUE LINE.	
"	6	—	In BLUE LINE. Heavy casualties in 'B' Coy. Capt. R.I. ROBSON M.C. killed. Two coys. move into our old front line. Enemy quieter.	
"	"	—	Dry & misty.	
"	7	—	In BLUE LINE. Relieved by 10th R. Innis. Fus. & went back to VLAMERTINGHE. Dry.	
VLAMERTINGHE	8	—	Showery. Nothing of note.	
"	9	—	Showery. Nothing of note.	
"	10	—	Great aerial activity. One of our planes drops into field	

WAR DIARY
or
INTELLIGENCE SUMMARY.
(Erase heading not required.)

Army Form C. 2118.

Place	Date	Hour	Summary of Events and Information	Remarks and references to Appendices
VLAMERTINGHE	1917 August 10		near by. Glorious weather.	
"	11		Company Commanders reconnoitre trenches. Very showery.	
"	12		Relieved 10th R. Innis. Fusiliers in BLACK LINE. Heavily shelled coming past St. JEAN. Showery.	
YPRES	13		In BLACK LINE. Quiet day. Heavy shelling on our right about 9 a.m. Dry. 2nd Lt. T. McROBERTS of "D" coy killed.	
"	14		In BLACK LINE. About 11.0 p.m. were relieved by 2 coys. of the 9th R. Innis. Fusiliers + 2 coys. of the 14th R. Ir. RIFLES. Entrained for VLAMERTINGHE at ASYLUM at 5 a.m. 15th inst. Dry.	
VLAMERTINGHE	15		Arrived in camp at 6.0 a.m. All ranks make off for sleep. Some of all the "push" material showery.	
"	16		Left camp at 1.0 a.m. + entrained for YPRES at 3.0 a.m. Zero day of Division push. Zero time 4.45 a.m. 107th Brigade in Divl. Reserve. 15th Battn. in LIVERPOOL TRENCH with Battn. H.Q. at VINERY. Assault of 108th + 109th Brigades not a success and they come back to BLACK LINE. At 6.0 p.m. C.O. called to Conference at Bde.	

Army Form C. 2118.

WAR DIARY
or
INTELLIGENCE SUMMARY.
(Erase heading not required.)

Instructions regarding War Diaries and Intelligence Summaries are contained in F. S. Regs., Part II. and the Staff Manual respectively. Title pages will be prepared in manuscript.

Place	Date	Hour	Summary of Events and Information	Remarks and references to Appendices
YPRES	1917 August 16		We relieve 8th Batt. in old British front line system with Bn. H.Q. at WIELTJE FARM. Glorious weather.	
"	17		Numbers of 61st Divn. officers reconnoitre our trenches. Relieved by 4th GLOUCESTERS. Come back to camp at VLAMERTINGHE. Great enemy aerial activity in back areas, causing serious casualties.	
VLAMERTINGHE	"		Several H.V. shells drop near camp. Dry.	
"	18		Repeated activity by enemy aeroplanes at night over our area. Bombs dropped near R.L.I. The enemy H.V. gun very active. Glorious weather.	
"	19		We take bus at 5.0 a.m. for WINNIZEELE area. Arrived in camp at 8.0 a.m. It looks like heaven. Glorious weather.	
WINNIZEELE	20		Aerial activity at night. Weather fine.	
"	21		Receive news of Divn. leaving 5th ARMY to join 3rd ARMY. Enemy aerial activity.	
"	22		Nothing of note.	
"	23		March at 5.0 a.m. to entrain at ESQUELBECQ. Entrain for	

WAR DIARY
or
INTELLIGENCE SUMMARY.

Army Form C. 2118.

Place	Date	Hour	Summary of Events and Information	Remarks and references to Appendices
Contd. WINNIZEELE	1917 August 23		BAPAUME at 8.0 a.m. Reach BAPAUME at 5.30 p.m. and march	
BARASTRE	24		to camp at BARASTRE. Showery weather	
"	25		Nothing of note.	
"	26		Advance party leaves for trenches held by South African Brigade in the TRESCAULT sector.	
"	27		Officers & N.C.O's visit trenches. Good weather.	
"	28		March from here to YTRES. Weather showery	
YTRES	29		Relieved 3rd (TRANSVAAL) SOUTH AFRICAN REGT. in TRESCAULT sector.	
"			Situation very quiet	
TRESCAULT sector	29		Situation very quiet. Work on trenches commenced	
"	30		Very quiet. Spasmodic shoot by Brigade on our left.	
"	31		Very quiet	

Montgomery Major
comdg 15th Bn Royal I. Rifles

WAR DIARY
or
INTELLIGENCE SUMMARY

Army Form C. 2118.

15 R I F Vol 24

Place	Date	Hour	Summary of Events and Information	Remarks and references to Appendices
In TRESCAULT Sector (Right Sub-sector)	1/9/17		Very quiet. Day.	
In TRESCAULT Sector	2/9/17		Weather fine. Situation quiet.	
In TRESCAULT Sector	3/9/17		Relieved in evening by 8/9th R.D. Rif. and proceed to Brigade Reserve at METZ. Draft of 108 O.R. (details from 8th and 9th R.A. Rif.) join Battalion.	
In Reserve at METZ	4/9/17		Weather fine	
	5/9/17		Weather very warm	
	6/9/17		Weather fine	
	7/9/17		Weather very fine	
	8/9/17		Weather fine	
	9/9/17		Move into Right Sub sector (TRESCAULT) to relieve 8/9 R.I.R. Front extended to "C" Sub (exclusive) to men Left (?) Lt.Col. C.G. Cole Hamilton, C.M.G., D.S.O. takes over command of the Battalion	
In Right Sub sector (TRESCAULT)	10/9/17		Weather fine. Situation quiet	
	11/9/17		" " "	
	12/9/17		" " "	

WAR DIARY
or
INTELLIGENCE SUMMARY.
(Erase heading not required).

Army Form C. 2118.

Place	Date	Hour	Summary of Events and Information	Remarks and references to Appendices
	13/9/17		In Right Subsector (TRESCAULT) Desultory fire. Situation quiet	
	14/9/17		" "	
	15/9/17		Relieved by 8/9th Bn. R.D. Rif. Proceeded to Billets	
			Reserve at EQUINCOURT	
	16/9/17		In Reserve at EQUINCOURT	Whilst out of the line the Coys. had Coys.
	17/9/17		" " Divisional Commander inspects the Battalion	
	18/9/17		" " Desultory fire	
	19/9/17		" " " "	
	20/9/17		" " " "	
	21/9/17		Moved into Right Sub-sector (TRESCAULT) to relieve 8/9th Bn. R.D. Rif.	
	22/9/17		In Right sub-sector (TRESCAULT) Desultory fire. Situation less quiet than	
			usual, enemy trench mortars active, enemy Artillery and Trench Mortars active	
	23/9/17		In Right sub-sector (TRESCAULT) Artillery and machine gun enemy about	
			10.20 p.m. on "B" Coy. Two of enemy seen at parapet but they	
			withdrew on being bombed	

WAR DIARY
or
INTELLIGENCE SUMMARY.
(Erase heading not required.)

Army Form C. 2118.

Place	Date	Hour	Summary of Events and Information	Remarks and references to Appendices
	24/9/17		In Right Bde. sector (TRESCAULT) Situation normal. Weather fine.	
	25/9/17		" " " "	
	26/9/17		" " " "	
	27/9/17		Relieved in Right Bde sector by 8/S.W.B.Rif. We relies to Brigade reserve at METZ. METZ has been shelled almost incessantly during the day but things became quiet about 7.30 p.m.	
	28/9/17		In Brigade reserve at METZ. No shelling of village to-day. Weather fine	
	29/9/17		" " " "	
	30/9/17		Whole Battalion to return home	Capt. J. Quinn, C.F. Joined 16 K.R. Royal Irish Rif

W.P.M[...] Lt. Col.
D/ 2/R.Ir.Rif.

WAR DIARY
INTELLIGENCE SUMMARY
Army Form C. 2118.

(Erase heading not required.)

Place	Date	Hour	Summary of Events and Information	Remarks and references to Appendices
	October 1st		In Brigade Reserve at METZ. Major W. A. Montgomery proceeds on leave, and Capt. E. F. Lepper takes over 2nd in command of Battalion.	
	2nd		In Reserve at METZ.	
	3rd		In Reserve at METZ. The Battalion is inspected in the morning by the Corps Commander. In the afternoon we relieve the 8/19th R.W. Rif. in the TRESCAULT Sector (Right Sub-sector)	
	4th		In TRESCAULT sector. Weather colder. Situation quiet.	
	5th		In TRESCAULT sector. Some rain. Situation quiet.	
	6th		In TRESCAULT sector. Weather very cold and wet. Situation quiet.	
	7th		In TRESCAULT sector. Weather windy, cold and wet. Situation quiet.	
	8th		In TRESCAULT sector. Weather cold and damp. An enemy patrol of 1 Officer and 8 Other Ranks attempted to enter "B" Sap close to the Sapping post at the head of the Sap. They were driven off leaving the Officer dead and one man slightly wounded. This occurred at 8.45 p.m.	
	9th		In TRESCAULT sector. Weather dry and warmer. Relieved by 9th R.W. Rif. and return to Divisional Reserve at EQUINCOURT.	

E. F. Lepper Capt
1st Bn Royal Irish Rifles
Comdg 15th R.I. Rif.

WAR DIARY
or
INTELLIGENCE SUMMARY.

Army Form C. 2118.

Place	Date	Hour	Summary of Events and Information	Remarks and references to Appendices
	10th		In Divisional Reserve at EQUINCOURT. Weather wet and cold	
	11th		" Weather cold and dry	
	12th		" Weather compact	
	13th		" Football Match – 15th R.R.Rif. versus 11th R.R.Rif. Score 3–2 in favour of opponents.	
	14th		2 Divisional Reserve at EQUINCOURT. Rugby Match – 15th R.R.Rif versus 10th R.R.Rif. Result – 11 points to nil in favour of opponents	
	15th		Relieved 8/9th R.R.Rif in TRESCAULT Sector (Right centre). Weather fine.	
	16th		TRESCAULT sector. Battn dry and very cold. Situation quiet	
	17th		" Situation quiet. Weather dry	
	18th		" Situation quiet. Weather dry and cold	
	19th		" Situation quiet. Weather cold	
	20th		" Weather dry and misty. Situation quiet	
	21st		Relieved in TRESCAULT sector by 5/9th R.R.Rif. Return to Brigade Reserve at METZ.	
	22nd		In Brigade reserve at METZ. Weather wet.	

Army Form C. 2118.

WAR DIARY
or
INTELLIGENCE SUMMARY.
(Erase heading not required.)

Instructions regarding War Diaries and Intelligence Summaries are contained in F. S. Regs., Part II. and the Staff Manual respectively. Title pages will be prepared in manuscript.

Place	Date	Hour	Summary of Events and Information	Remarks and references to Appendices
	23rd		In Brigade Reserve at METZ. Weather dry.	
	24th		" " Weather milder and wet.	
	25th		" " Weather very wet.	
	26th		" " Weather cold and wet.	
	27th		Relieved 2/17th R.B. Rif. in TRESCAULT sector (Right Subsector) HAVRINCOURT WOOD shelled during the afternoon. No casualties.	f.Lt.Col Barraclough Lewis left, 15th Bn. Roy. Fus. shew comm.
	28th		In TRESCAULT Sector. Situation normal. Weather very cold.	
	29th		" Enemy artillery fire increasing. Bay in STAFFORD TRENCH (Head of QUEENS LANE) held as L.G. post destroyed during night.	
	30th		In TRESCAULT sector. Situation normal. Weather milder.	
	31st		In TRESCAULT sector. Enemy artillery heavy on Front Line during the day. Weather dry.	

W.R.M[signature]
Lt. Col.
Co. 15th R.W. Rif.

2nd Nov. 1917.

107/36/15 R Irish Rifles Vol 26

Army Form C. 2118.

WAR DIARY
or
INTELLIGENCE SUMMARY.
(Erase heading not required.)

Place	Date	Hour	Summary of Events and Information	Remarks and references to Appendices
N. of TRESCAULT	1.11.17		In trenches. Nothing of importance	
	2.11.17		Relieved by 8/9th R. Ir. Rifs. Went into Divisional Reserve at VAULLART WOOD camp. Weather bad + mud everywhere.	
YPRES	3.11.17		Routine inspections. Nothing of note	
	4.11.17		Rumours of coming push. Increased activity in rear areas.	
	5.11.17		Lewis Gun + Signalling Classes commenced work. 2/Lt. D.G. McGillow joined as reinforcement. 2/Lt. A.W.F. Gilmore returned from leave	
	6.11.17		Doctor commenced Stretcher-bearer class in view of coming push. 15th unbeaten in football competitions (Wilkycombe Cup) to date	
	7.11.17		2/Lts F. Money, F.J. Ritter, L. Addy joined Batt⁵ today.	
N. of TRESCAULT	8.11.17		Went into line this evg. Weather very misty. Kelly's Ridge has been hit by 77 mm. Shell during 8/9th hour. H. Qrs dug-out very comfortable now	
	9.11.17		Nothing of note. Usual trench routine & activity.	
	10.11.17			
	11.11.17			

WAR DIARY
or
INTELLIGENCE SUMMARY.
(Erase heading not required.)

Army Form C. 2118.

Place	Date	Hour	Summary of Events and Information	Remarks and references to Appendices
N. of TRESCAULT	12.11.17		Enemy shelled front line heavily about 10.0 p.m.	
	13.11.17		Relieved by 8/9d R.B. Rifles	
METZ	14.11.17		Preparing for "push". 2/Lt B. Stone, 2/Lt L. Farrell, V.C. Vivian, 2/Lt W. Kinny joined Battn for duty & were posted to A, B, C, D coys respectively.	
"	15.11.17		Officers reconnoitred Armies area.	
"	16.11.17		2/Lt G.E.S. Gordon becomes act. Captain whilst commdg "D" Coy. Much discussion as to results of above. Football match with 8/9d tomorrow.	
	17.11.17		8/9 win match by 7 goals to 1. Very exciting match. Played at YPRES. Tanks coming through METZ at night in large numbers. Road of traffic incessant	
YPRES	18.11.17		Moved to camp opposite LITTLE WOOD, YPRES. Preparations for "push" nearly complete	
"	19.11.17		Incessant work all day. Everyone in high spirits. After dark 51st Divn commenced moving up to the line along road outside camp. Battn to move before dawn to forward	

Army Form C. 2118.

WAR DIARY
or
INTELLIGENCE SUMMARY.
(Erase heading not required.)

Instructions regarding War Diaries and Intelligence Summaries are contained in F. S. Regs., Part II. and the Staff Manual respectively. Title pages will be prepared in manuscript.

Place	Date	Hour	Summary of Events and Information	Remarks and references to Appendices
YPRES	19.11.17		area.	
	20.11.17		Moved out for line at 5.30 a.m. with Major H.A. Montgomery D.S.O. in command. Details left out of battle go to camp near VELU WOOD.	
	From 20/11/1917 to 27/11/1917 is covered by Narrative & operation orders attached.			
BERKSHIRE	28/11/17		Battⁿ resting	
"	29/11/17		Marched to YPRES station & entrained for FOSSEAUX area. Detrained at RIVIERE & marched to BERNEVILLE. Prospects of a rest. Arrived at BERNEVILLE at 3.0 p.m. fairly good billets.	
BERNEVILLE	30/11/17		Received orders to march at half-an-hour's notice back to the line. Marched out at 10.30 a.m. destination for the day being COURCELLES-LE-COMTE where the night was spent.	

M.Montgomery Major
for Lieut-Colonel
Comm^g 13 (S) Bⁿ Royal Irish Rifles

SECRET.   Copy No.......

                    Operation Order No. 26
                              by
         Lieut. Col. C.G. COLE-HAMILTON C.M.G., D.S.O.,
              Commanding 15th. (S) Bn. Royal Irish Rifles.

                                              18th. November 1917.

         Reference Map : 57 C N.E.
                         57 C S.E.

1.   The 15th. Bn. Royal Irish Rifles will move to Concentration Area at P.4.a.5.8. on the morning of the 20th. Inst. via RUYAULCOURT and P.4. C & A.
     The Starting Point for the Brigade will be road junction P.20.B.8.9.

2.   Companies will be on parade in 'A' and 'B' Companies Camp, ready to march at 5-30.a.m.

3.   <u>Dress : Battle Order.</u> Company Commanders will hand a certificate to the Adjutant before marching off, stating that the men's packs contain nothing but the kit laid down in 107th. Brigade Appendix I - Dress and Equipment.

4.   All blankets must be rolled in bundles of 10, labelled and stacked in one hut per ~~Company~~ Camp near the Road half an hour before Companies leave their Camps. Officers' Valises will be packed and placed in the same hut.
     The Officers' Valises and blankets of Details will be packed and placed in a separate hut.
     A guard of two men per hut will be found from the details.
     Transport will collect these blankets.

5.   <u>MEALS, RATIONS ETC.</u> Breakfast before starting, Dinner not later than 11 a.m. on Concentration Area ground.
     Before leaving Assembly Point each man will receive a full day's rations. He will then be in possession of unconsumed portion of to-morrow's rations, a full day's rations and an Iron Ration.
     Water bottles must be filled before leaving this Camp.
     A certificate will be handed to Adjutant by Company Commanders at Assembly Point that all ranks of their Companies are complete as stated in this paragraph.

6.   <u>AMMUNITION ETC.</u> The amount of ammunition to be carried on the man will be completed at Concentration Area.

7.   <u>LEWIS GUNS AND MAGAZINES.</u> These will be carried by limbers to Concentration Area.

8.   <u>DETAILS.</u> All Officers', N.C.O's and men left out of battle will parade outside Orderly Room.
     The Assistant Adjutant will march the party to the Detail Camp at VELU I.29.d.7.3. Hour to be notified later.

9.   Lieut. J. ENGLISH'S Brigade Carrying Party will march in rear of the Battalion.

10. No. 15/44810 Corporal PILBEAM 'C' Coy. and No. 15/43256 L/Corpl. HIRST 'D' Company will report to Lieut. TOOLEY 10th. R. Ir. Rif. at 8 a.m. at J.34.c.9.0.

Transport will be brigaded and march in rear of Brigade.

A C K N O W L E D G E.

(Sd) J.J. STEWART Captain & Adjutant,

15th. (S) Bn. Royal Irish Rifles.

Issued at 3-45.p.m. by Runner.

Copy No. 1. - Commanding Officer.
" No. 2. Second-in-Command.
" No. 3. Battalion Headquarters.
" No. 4. O.C. 'A' Company.
" No. 5. O.C. 'B' "
" No. 6. O.C. 'C' "
" No. 7. O.C. 'D' "
" No. 8. Quartermaster.
" No. 9. Transport Officer.
" No. 10. File.

SECRET.   Copy No........

15th. (S) Bn. Royal Irish Rifles.

Operation Order No. 30.

Reference Map : MOEUVRES 1/20,000.

The Offensive will be resumed to-day by the IV Corps.
The 40th. Division on our right will attack BOURLON WOOD and Village.
The 36th. Division will attack on its present front and 56th. Division will co-operate on left.
The Attack on the 36th. Division Front will be carried out in two phases :-
The first phase Zero 10-30.a.m.
The Second "   "   1 p.m.
Six tanks (three pairs) will co-operate on front E.22.d.central to CANAL.
Two of these tanks will start between HINDENBURG trenches due East of E.22.central at 10-30.a.m. (Zero First Phase). They will work Northwards and Westwards between the trenches until the CANAL is reached.

TASK OF BATTALION.
1.   Co-operate with tanks between HINDENBURG trenches taking, mopping up and picketing all Strong Points and trenches in HINDENBURG System from starting point of tanks on right to CANAL.
2.   Form defensive flank facing West on CANAL.

DISPOSITIONS.
Companies will be formed up in their present positions facing East and North East, ready to get out of the trenches and follow tanks by 9-45.a.m.   *quickly*
Report when Companies are in position will be rendered to Adjutant by following words :-
'A' Company   "BASS".
'B'   "   "STOUT".
'C'   "   "IS".
'D'   "   "BEST".

METHOD.
Companies will get out of their trenches in succession Northwards and Westwards from 'A' Company, and follow the tanks at a distance of 100 yards.
There will be no leap-frog.
'A' Company will follow the tanks to CANAL and will there find a platoon to form a defensive flank facing West.
Companies following the leading Company must closely support it throughout its advance.   When CANAL is reached the Northern and Eastern trench line will then be occupied.
One machine gun will go forward for co-operation with defensive flank when formed.
The 10th. Battalion will support the 15th. Battalion.
All ranks must be emphatically warned of the absolute necessity of immediately mopping up and placing sentries over all dugouts, Strong Points, Communication Trenches etc.   Men so posted must be told that their job is "to cork the bottle safely" until it can be thoroughly mopped up inside etc. by formed parties.

BATTALION HEADQUARTERS.   will be at 'A' Company's original Headquarters in this sector.

COMMAND POST.   will be pushed forward as far as possible.

ACKNOWLEDGE.

23rd. Nov. 1917.   (Sd) JOHN H. STEWART Captain & Adjutant,
                        15th. (S) Bn. Royal Irish Rifles.

Issued at 8 a.m. by Runner.

Copy No. 1.   O.C. 'A' Company.
 "   No. 2.   O.C. 'B'   "
 "   No. 3.   O.C. 'C'   "
 "   No. 4.   O.C. 'D'   "
 "   No. 5.   10th. Royal Irish Rifles.
 "   No. 6.   107th. Infantry Brigade.
 "   No. 7.   File.

SECRET.   Copy No. ....

15th. (S) Bn. Royal Irish Rifles Order No. 31.
****

                                                24th. November 1917.

   The 1st. Bn. Royal Irish Fusiliers will relieve the Battalion in its present position this morning as under :-

'D' Coy. 1st. R. Ir. Fus. will relieve 'D' Coy. 15th. R. Ir. Rif.
'C' "   -do-   -do-   'C' "   -do-
'A' "   -do-   -do-   'B' "   -do-
'B' "   -do-   -do-   'A' "   -do-

   Relief will be effected in the order detailed above.
   On relief 15th. Bn. Royal Irish Rifles will withdraw Southwards down HINDENBURG SUPPORT TRENCH in order from North to South 'D', 'C', 'B', 'A'.
   'D' Company 15th. Bn. Royal Irish Rifles will be in touch with 'B' Company 1st. Royal Irish Fusiliers.

   Completion of relief will be notified to Battalion Headquarters.

                A C K N O W L E D G E.

                           (Sd) JOHN H. STEWART Captain & Adjt.,
                                15th. (S) Bn. Royal Irish Rifles.

Issued at 11.45 A.M. by Runner.

Copy No. 1. O.C. 'A' Company.
  "   No. 2. O.C. 'B'   "
  "   No. 3. O.C. 'C'   "
  "   No. 4. O.C. 'D'   "
  "   No. 5. 1st. Bn. Royal Irish Fusiliers.
  "   No. 6. File.

SECRET.   Copy No. ......

15th. (S) Bn. Royal Irish Rifles Order No. 32.

24th. November 1917.

Reference Map : MOEUVRES 1/20,000.

The HINDENBURG SUPPORT TRENCHES West of E.22.a.45.55.,- E.22.a.60.90. will be attacked to-day by the 1st. Bn. Royal Irish Fusiliers supported by the 15th. Bn. Royal Irish Rifles and the 10th. Bn. Royal Irish Rifles less two Companies.
The attack will be delivered from the East.

ASSEMBLY.
The troops taking part will be formed up in HINDENBURG SUPPORT TRENCH in order from North to South 1st. R. Ir. Fus., 15th. R. Ir. Rif., 10th. R. Ir. Rif. less two Companies.

ARTILLERY.
Both heavy and field artillery will co-operate.
A bombardment will be opened on trenches to be attacked at Zero - 20.
At Zero - 3 known enemy Strong Points will be subjected to a hurricane Stokes Mortar bombardment by 107th. Trench Mortar Battery.
At Zero barrage will lift Westwards at rate of 100 yards in 10 minutes, when the 1st. Bn. Royal Irish Fusiliers will attack over the open.
The 15th. Bn. Royal Irish Rifles will closely support the 1st. Bn. Royal Irish Fusiliers and follow their advance.
In the event of the 1st. Bn. Royal Irish Fusiliers reaching their objective on the CANAL, it is expected that they would then be strong enough to hold enemy trenches West of SUNKEN ROAD in E.15 d and E.21.b.   In this case the boundary between the 1st. Bn. Royal Irish Fusiliers and 15th. Bn. Royal Irish Rifles will be this Road. But at all times after the attack the Right flank of the 1st. Bn. Royal Irish Fusiliers facing Northwards will always be the left flank of the 15th. Bn. Royal Irish Rifles also facing Northwards.

BATTALION HEADQUARTERS.
1st. R. Ir. Fus. and 15th. R. Ir. Rif. - E.22.c.95.10.

COMMAND POST.   will be established at Zero 300 yards East of block and will follow the advance.

ZERO.   Zero - 3-30.p.m.

A C K N O W L E D G E.

(Sd) JOHN H. STEWART Captain & Adjutant,
15th. (S) Bn. Royal Irish Rifles.

Issued at 11-30.a.m.

Copies No. 1 to 4.   Companies.
Copy No. 5. 1st. Royal Irish Fusiliers.
"   No. 6. 10th. Royal Irish Rifles.
"   No. 7. File.

15th. (S) Bn. Royal Irish Rifles.

NARRATIVE

Covering Operations 20th. to 27th. November 1917.

Reference Map : MOEUVRES Special Sheet 1/20,000 Edition 5 F.

20th. November 1917.

(Zero day - Zero Hour 6-20.a.m.)
The Battalion moved to its Concentration Area at P.4.a.5.5. arriving at 8-30.a.m.   Dinners at 11 a.m.
Battalion here fully equipped in Battle Order (Battalion Order No. 26 dated 19-11-17 attached).
At 1 p.m. the Battalion moved to new position of readiness at K.26.c.Central.   Raining heavily, blowing hard and very cold.   Battalion Headquarters established in a shell-hole.
8-20.p.m. Battalion crossed single-man wooden bridge over Canal due NORD at K.26.c.7.2.   Arrived in HAVRINCOURT at 1 a.m. 21st. November 1917.   Battalion disposed in cellars and other shelters close to trenches.

21st. November 1917.

Commanding Officer attended Brigadier General's Conference.
Battalion held in readiness to move at 8 a.m., later instructed not move before noon, later prepared to move at 10 minutes notice.
3-30.p.m. Moved to HINDENBURG SUPPORT at K.4.c. and K.4.d., with Battalion Headquarters at K.4.d.15.50., arriving at 6-30.p.m. Night was spent here.

22nd. November 1917.

Commanding Officer attended Brigadier General's Conference at 4-30.a.m. when attack on HINDENBURG SUPPORT from E.22.c.90.20. through E.22.central - E.22.a. and Westwards to CANAL was discussed.
At 7-15.a.m. Commanding Officer returned to Battalion Headquarters and issued orders to Battalion for this attack.
8-15.a.m. Battalion moved up to position for attack, head of leading Company ('A') at E.28.b.10.80.
Zero Hour 11 a.m.   Advance proceeded well until E.22.a. central was reached when the then leading Company ('B') was held up by heavy machine gun fire from enemy Strong Points.   One of these at E.22.a.50.90. which appeared to be most seriously hampering the advance was attacked from the flanks by Platoons from 'C' and 'D' Companies.   By 1 p.m. both these Platoons had been beaten back into the trench and had sustained heavy casualties.   O.C. 'B' Company (2/Lieut. O.H. JONES) was about the same time mortally wounded whilst gallantly endeavouring to get his Company further Westward along the line of the trench.
About 1-30.p.m. the enemy counter-attacked and in fierce and close fighting which ensued we sustained further heavy casualties, among which were 2/Lieut. H.J. BUCHANAN (Missing believed Killed) 2/Lieuts. G.A. McFARLAND, W.J. CORDNER and V.C. VINSEN (Wounded).
The counter-attack was repulsed after heavy fighting, and our left was established at E.22.a.45.45. where a block was made at junction of HINDENBURG SUPPORT with Communication Trench leading to Strong Point at E.22.a.50.90.   This position was held by us throughout our occupation of the line in spite of heavy fire and repeated efforts on the part of the enemy to dislodge us.   Captain J.E.S. CONDON in particular did excellent work throughout at this point.

23rd. November 1917.

Commanding Officer called to Brigade for Conference at 4-30.a.m., and returned at 7 a.m. Held Company Commander's Conference and issued Order No. 30 (Copy attached). Battalion Headquarters moved to E.22.b.95.15.

Only one of our tanks reached vicinity of their Assembly position, and was then about 15 minutes after Zero.

'A' Company, as detailed, was seen to follow in the wake of this tank in good order and well in hand.

The tank however did not proceed in the direction laid down, but sheared off Eastwards towards BOURLON WOOD, thus leaving 'A' Company quite unsupported in a critical position hemmed in by enemy Strong Points. This Company suffered heavily, but one of its Platoons (No. I) took one Strong Point at E.22.d.80.80., where they killed many of the enemy and took 12 prisoners. 2/Lieut. R.H. RANKIN was killed and 2/Lieut. H.C. GRIGG was wounded in this little attack. The Platoon carried on steadily under the senior surviving N.C.O., sending runners through to Battalion Headquarters who were able to state exactly where the Platoon had got to, and maintained touch throughout the day and into the night, when the 10th. Royal Irish Rifles established the line slightly in front of their position. The conduct throughout of this Platoon was excellent.

Meanwhile the other two Platoons under their Company Commander (Captain P.M. MILLER) were holding on grimly at about E.22.b.20.20. taking casualties freely, as they were exposed to the fire of at least two enemy Strong Points. They held on all day, but succeeded in extricating themselves at dusk. They maintained touch by runner throughout the day with Battalion Headquarters, although they had several casualties to runners. 2/Lieut. J. MARSH was killed in this position.

2/Lieut. A.W.F. GILMORE M.C. when endeavouring to locate No. I Platoon missed their post in the dark, and blundered into an enemy outpost in a position which we had been advised was held by the unit on our right. He is Missing since this time. He fell on being fired on, and no movement of his body was observed by the N.C.O. who accompanied him, and who subsequently got back to our line.

24th. November 1917.

At 11-30.a.m. the enemy counter-attacked our trench at E.22.a.90.40. About 60 of the enemy with Light Machine Gun Detachment pressed their attack with great determination. They were practically destroyed. It is believed that only two of the whole party regained the enemy's line. One Light Machine Gun, identification and documents from several bodies remained in our hands. We took no prisoners, wounded or otherwise.

At 1 p.m. the 1st. Royal Irish Fusiliers relieved us in trench (see Order No. 31 attached.)

From 1-30.p.m. to 2-30.p.m. the enemy subjected our trench to a heavy bombardment, and later were observed concentrating to the N.E. of our position. From 2-45.p.m. until 4-30.p.m. there was heavy and continuous Artillery fire on our front. The 1st. Royal Irish Fusiliers and we in a much lesser degree took many casualties from shell fire whilst waiting to carry out the Operation as detailed in Order No. 32 (copy attached)

This attack did not take place, and at 7.p.m. we were relieved by the 10th. Bn. Royal Irish Rifles and withdrew into Brigade Reserve in KANGAROO ALLEY E.28.b.4.8. to K.3.a.90.80. with Battalion Headquarters at K.28.b.4.1.

25th. November 1917.

A quiet day for us spent in KANGAROO ALLEY. No casualties.

26th. November 1917.

        Still in KANGAROO ALLEY.   Received orders that we were to be relieved by unit of 108th. Infantry Brigade, this cancelled, and relief by 22nd. Royal Fusiliers commenced.

27th. November 1917.

        We are relieved at 1 a.m. and withdraw to positions in old British Front Line in K. 13 and 14, with Battalion Headquarters at K.13.b.90.30.
        At 4 p.m. Battalion relieved by Battalion Royal Fusiliers, and on relief withdrew to BARASTRE where we arrived in Camp (Huts) about 6-30.p.m.

9th. Dec. 1917.   *W.H. Montgomery*   Major,
    for Officer Commanding 15th. (S) Bn. Royal Itish Rifles.

WAR DIARY
or
INTELLIGENCE SUMMARY.
(Erase heading not required.)

Army Form C. 2118.

15 R. Irish Rifles

VII 27

Place	Date	Hour	Summary of Events and Information	Remarks and references to Appendices
	1917			
COURCELLES-EN-GOMOIS	Dec. 1		The Battalion moves to Beaulencourt via Achiet-le-Grand and	
BEAULENCOURT	" 2		BAPAUME. Arrived at 5.30 p.m.	
			The Battalion marches via Rocquigny and Bus to camp near YTRES. Arrived at 2 p.m. Battalion stands by ready to move at an hours notice	
YTRES	" 3		Battalion ready to move at an hours notice. Uneventful day.	
YTRES	" 4		We move at 12 noon to take up area as support Battalion of 107th Brigade (Divisional Reserve) in Havrincourt Wood. Battalion all under canvas. Weather very cold.	
HAVRINCOURT WOOD	" 5		Uneventful day. Weather still cold.	
"	" 6		Parties of officers reconnoitre trenches held by 108th & 109th Brigades	
"	" 7		We receive orders to relieve 14th R. Irish Rifles in support of 109th Brigade and to be counter-attack Battalion whilst in that position	
HAVRINCOURT WOOD	" 8		We relieve 14th R. Irish Rifles in Gonnelieu Sector. The enemy fairly active with artillery on roads and C.T.s	
GONNELIEU SECTOR	" 9		Enemy artillery active. Trenches cleaned and fire steps dug	
"	" 10		Enemy aircraft fly low over our lines in the morning. Our own and	

Army Form C. 2118.

WAR DIARY
or
INTELLIGENCE SUMMARY.
(Erase heading not required.)

Instructions regarding War Diaries and Intelligence Summaries are contained in F. S. Regs., Part II. and the Staff Manual respectively. Title pages will be prepared in manuscript.

Place	Date	Hour	Summary of Events and Information	Remarks and references to Appendices
	17			
GONNELIEU Sector	Dec 10		enemy artillery active in afternoon. Ration Dump heavily shelled at 6 p.m.	
"	..11		We are ordered to relieve the 10th R. Irish Rifles in the Right Sub-sector on the evening of the 12th. Officers reconnoitre their line.	
"	..12		Uneventful day. We relieve 10th R. Irish Rifles. Relief completed at 7 p.m. Enemy artillery active on 6 to and Ration Dump.	
"	..13		Parties of officers of R.N. Division reconnoitre our line. Day uneventful.	
"	..14		The enemy shell our Battalion Headquarters heavily at 4 a.m. We are relieved by Nelson Battalion of R.N.D. and withdraw to METZ-EN-COUTURE. Arrive in METZ at 12 midnight.	
METZ-EN-COUTURE	..15		We move to ETRICOURT at 1 p.m. via FINS and EQUANCOURT. Battalion under canvas. Weather very cold.	
ETRICOURT	..16		Uneventful day. Weather very cold with heavy downfall of snow at night.	
ETRICOURT	..17		We entrain for DOULLENS area. We arrive at Mondicourt at 4 p.m. We march to GRAND ROULLECOURT via LECHEUX. Marching very difficult	

WAR DIARY
or
INTELLIGENCE SUMMARY.
(Erase heading not required.)

Army Form C. 2118.

Place	Date	Hour	Summary of Events and Information	Remarks and references to Appendices
GRAND RULLECOURT	Dec 18		owing to snow on roads. All Battalion in Billets.	
"	19		All Battalion works on roads to clear them for traffic. Our transport arrives at 10 p.m. after a very trying journey. Training started. Weather still very cold.	
"	20		Uneventful	
"	21		Uneventful	
"	22		Weather very cold.	
"	23		Uneventful	
"	24		Preparations for Xmas dinner	
"	25		All ranks have a very merry Xmas	
"	26		We receive orders to move to CORBIE area on 27th inst.	
"	27		We march from G. RULLECOURT at 6 a.m. and entrain at 9 a.m. at MONDICOURT. We arrive in CORBIE at 2 p.m. and march to adjoining village of LA NEUVILLE. All Battalion in Billets	
LA NEUVILLE	28		Training proceeding	
"	29		Uneventful	

Army Form C. 2118.

WAR DIARY
or
INTELLIGENCE SUMMARY.
(Erase heading not required.)

Instructions regarding War Diaries and Intelligence Summaries are contained in F. S. Regs., Part II. and the Staff Manual respectively. Title pages will be prepared in manuscript.

Place	Date	Hour	Summary of Events and Information	Remarks and references to Appendices
LA NEUVILLE	Dec 30		Uneventful	E.L.C Hamilton
"	Dec 31		Uneventful	

A6945. Wt. W14422/M160 350,000 12/16 D. D. & L. Forms/C. 2118/14.

Jan-Feb 1918

Army Form C. 2118.

WAR DIARY
or
INTELLIGENCE SUMMARY.
(Erase heading not required.)

Instructions regarding War Diaries and Intelligence Summaries are contained in F. S. Regs., Part II. and the Staff Manual respectively. Title pages will be prepared in manuscript.

15- R. Irish Rifles

Vol 28

Place	Date 1918 January	Hour	Summary of Events and Information	Remarks and references to Appendices
LA NEUVILLE.	1		Battn. resting in billets.	
"	2		" " "	
"	3		" " "	
"	4		" " " — Capt. R.W. Millar and Capt. J.J. Hill awarded the Military Cross.	
"	5		" " " — Capt. J.H. Stewart and R.Q.M.S. Thornton, awarded the Military Cross.	
"	6		" " " — Capt. R.W. Millar and Capt. J.S. Condon, awarded the Military Cross.	
"	7		Battn. marched to Proyart 2.2.2.15 in Proyart.	
PROYART.	8		Battn. in billets.	
"	9		Battn. marched to Curchy.	
CURCHY.	10		Battn. in billets.	
"	11		Battn. marched to Pithon.	
PITHON.	12		Battn. marched to Brigade Reserve in Fontaine Les Clercs. Dugouts.	
FONTAINE LES CLERCS.	13		Battn. in Brigade Reserve.	
"	14		" " " "	
"	15		" " " "	
"	16		" " " "	
"	17		" " " "	
"	18		Battn. relieved 8/9th Royal Irish Rifles in Right Subsector. St. Quentin.	
"	19		Battn. in Right Subsector. Trenches in bad condition. No ambuscades at resetting. Patrols.	
GRUGIES.	20		" " Work on trenches commenced.	

Army Form C. 2118.

WAR DIARY
or
INTELLIGENCE SUMMARY.
(Erase heading not required.)

Instructions regarding War Diaries and Intelligence Summaries are contained in F. S. Regs. Part II. and the Staff Manual respectively. Title pages will be prepared in manuscript.

Place	Date 1918 January	Hour	Summary of Events and Information	Remarks and references to Appendices
GRUGIES.	21		Batt. in RIGHT SUBSECTOR. Patrols.	
"	22		Enemy patrol entered our trenches at MIDNIGHT 21/22ND, and captured one man (severely wounded) and succeeded in wounding an N.C.O and 3 men. They started the LIAISON post of RIGHT Coy. but approached along front line trench from the Bn. on the RIGHT.	
"	23		Batt. in RIGHT SUBSECTOR. On night of 22/23RD the enemy raided a s.p. on the Batt. on the RIGHT and the 15th Batt. Stood To. Our front remained quiet.	
"	24		Batt. in RIGHT SUBSECTOR. Relieved at night by 8/9th Royal Irish Rifles and moved into BRIGADE SUPPORT in dugouts in GRUGIES.	
"	25		Batt. in BRIGADE SUPPORT.	
"	26		" Aerial activity commenced.	
"	27		" Two escaping German prisoners captured while attempting to get through our wire in LEFT SUBSECTOR. Much activity in the air on both sides.	
"	28		Batt. in BRIGADE SUPPORT. Enemy planes very active all day. Scout of 54th Squadron forced to land at Fort Vfy.	
"	29		" Aerial activity.	
"	30		" (Relieved 8/9th Royal Irish Rifles in RIGHT SUBSECTOR at night.	
"	31		Batt. in RIGHT SUBSECTOR. Greatcoats of the German prisoners who attempted to escape were found behind our front line.	

W. Montgomery Hughes
Cmdg. 15th Batt. R. I. Rifles

WAR DIARY
or
INTELLIGENCE SUMMARY.

(Erase heading not required.)

Army Form C. 2118.

15 R Irish Rifles

Vol 29

Instructions regarding War Diaries and Intelligence Summaries are contained in F. S. Regs., Part II. and the Staff Manual respectively. Title pages will be prepared in manuscript.

Place	Date 1918.	Hour	Summary of Events and Information	Remarks and references to Appendices
GRUGIES	February 1st		Battn. in RIGHT SUBSECTOR. Weather very cold with severe frost.	
	2nd		Battn. in RIGHT SUBSECTOR. Frost.	
	3rd		Battn. in RIGHT SUBSECTOR. Weather very cold. Aerial activity.	
	4th		Battn. in RIGHT SUBSECTOR. Weather very cold.	
	5th		Battn. in RIGHT SUBSECTOR. Enemy artillery very active. Weather dry.	
	6th		Battn. in RIGHT SUBSECTOR. Weather fine.	
	7th		Battn. in RIGHT SUBSECTOR. Weather mild.	
	8th		Battn. in RIGHT SUBSECTOR. Weather mild. Relieved in evening by 1st Bn. Royal Irish Rifles.	
	9th		Battn. in BRIGADE SUPPORT. Weather cold.	
	10th		Battn. in BRIGADE SUPPORT. Weather cold. Relieved 10th Bn. Royal Irish Rifles in Battn. RESERVE in evening	
	11th		Battn. in BRIGADE RESERVE. Weather fine. Preparations for raid.	
	12th		Battn. in BRIGADE RESERVE. Weather fine. Preparations for raid.	
	13th		Battn. in BRIGADE RESERVE. Weather very cold and wet. Preparations for raid.	
	14th		Battn. in BRIGADE RESERVE. Weather fine. At 7pm a party of 3 Officers and 31 O.R. left our lines at P.P.7. and attempted to raid a post in the enemies lines at B.7.c.55.45. They found the posts standing to, and as it was a silent raid they were unable to get through the wire at the post. Two attempts were made, and the enemy turned a Light M.G. The party withdrew at 1-30 a.m. No casualties.	
	15th		Battn. in BRIGADE RESERVE. Weather fine. Relieved in the evening by the 2nd Bn Inniskillings Fusiliers, and moved in DIVISIONAL RESERVE in billets in Cr. SERRUCOURT.	
Cr. SERRUCOURT	16th		Battn. in DIVISIONAL RESERVE. Weather very fine. Battn. on working parties.	
	17th		Battn. in DIVISIONAL RESERVE. Weather fine. Working parties.	
	18th		Battn. in DIVISIONAL RESERVE. Weather fine. Bn. working in Battle Zone.	
	19th		Battn. in DIVISIONAL RESERVE. Weather fine. Bn. working in Battle Zone.	
	20th		Battn. in DIVISIONAL RESERVE. Weather fine. Bn. working in Battle Zone.	

Army Form C. 2118.

WAR DIARY
or
INTELLIGENCE SUMMARY.
(Erase heading not required.)

Instructions regarding War Diaries and Intelligence
Summaries are contained in F. S. Regs., Part II.
and the Staff Manual respectively. Title pages
will be prepared in manuscript.

Place	Date 1918.	Hour	Summary of Events and Information	Remarks and references to Appendices
Gd SERAPCOURT	February 21st 22nd		Batt. in DIVISIONAL RESERVE. Weather fine. Softy on Rifle Range. Batt. in DIVISIONAL RESERVE. Weather murky. Batt. relieved the 9th Royal Irish Fusiliers in the evening in the CENTRE SUBSECTOR. Patrols.	
ST. QUENTIN.	23rd 24th 25th		Batt. in CENTRE SECTOR. Weather cleared up. Patrols. Batt. in CENTRE SECTOR. Weather misty. Patrols. Batt. in CENTRE SECTOR. Weather misty. Patrols. A party of the enemy about 12 strong attempted to enter No.2. Sap at 5.20 a.m but were driven off. Several bombs were thrown, and two of our men were wounded.	
	26th 27th		Batt. in CENTRE SECTOR. Weather very fine. Patrols. Batt. in CENTRE SECTOR. Weather fine. At 4.30 a.m a German Patrol about 10 strong marched one of our advanced saps, they were driven off by our rifle fire, leaving a prisoner dead in our hands. He was a 2/Cpl. belonging to the 5th Grenadier Regiment, 36th Division, and was wearing the Iron Cross ribbon.	
	28th		Batt. in CENTRE SUBSECTOR. Weather fine. Batt. "stood to" in the afternoon. No attack. Relieved at night by 12th Bn Royal Irish Rifles and moved into Billets in Gd. SERAPCOURT. Brigade Reserve.	

E. J. Zeppel Major.

Commanding 1st & 2nd the Royal Irish Rifles.

107th Brigade.

36th Division.

15th BATTALION

THE ROYAL IRISH RIFLES

MARCH 1918

15th Battalion Royal Irish Rifles

War Diary March 1st to 20th 1918

is missing.

15th Batt - Royal 2nd Rifles

107/36

J.S 30

WAR DIARY
INTELLIGENCE SUMMARY.
(Erase heading not required.)

Army Form C. 2118.

Place	Date 1918 March	Hour	Summary of Events and Information	Remarks and references to Appendices
AUBIGNY	21/22		The rear now deals with the movements of the Batt" details which consisted of transport personnel Quartermaster Stores, personal effects on of action, Who rendered armory parts from Divl Supplied, hospital baptis with it wagk of some 100 O.R. which arrived to-day. The Batt" itself was gone, killed, wounded and prisoners. Capt P.M. MILLER M.C. commanded the little party.	
CANAL BANK	22/23		Occupied detached the line behind the village.	
BROUCHY	23/24		Do	
GUISCARD	24/25			
GUERBIGNY	25/26			
ERCHES	26	6.30 p.m	Took up position in old British Trench, behind ERCHES, 1st Batt R. Irish Rifles on our right and a Company of Royal Engineers on our left. One Machine Gun and section who attacked b-us.	
		9 p.m	A patrol of 6 O.Rs under 2nd Lieut. BOYD went out towards the two roads leading into ERCHES from ANDECHY and LE QUESNOY and to give warning of approach of enemy. Another outpost has been sent out at 7 p.m. to N.E. corner of ERCHES. The second patrol had just arrived at its post when both were attacked by about 50 of the enemy and were driven in.	
		10 p.m	A party of the enemy about 20 strong and more or less intoxicated was discovered outing to the noise they made outside the wire N. of ERCHES. On being challenged they replied in French and English. Suspecting a ruse we again challenged them both in French and English and getting no reply, we opened fire on them wounding several. Patrol then withdrew.	

A. Winter Anderson Lieut Acty
for O.C. 15th Bn R Royal Rifles

WAR DIARY

INTELLIGENCE SUMMARY

15th Bn. Royal Irish Rifles

Army Form C. 2118.

Place	Date 1918 March	Hour	Summary of Events and Information	Remarks and references to Appendices
	27	5 a.m.	A French Cavalry patrol came up from ARVILLERS and intended proceeding to ERCHES. The officer in command was informed that the latter place was in the hands of the enemy. Soon after a German cavalry patrol (5 strong) came up from behind our lines. We killed one and wounded another and the remainder rode away.	
		8 a.m.	With daylight enemy artillery and machine guns became very active. After a preliminary bombardment with T.Ms. and rifle grenades enemy made a bombing attack on our right causing several casualties but who driven out by 2nd Lieut YOUNG and a handful of men. Meanwhile we had only with rifles.	
		12 noon	All through the day our position was bombarded with artillery and T.Ms. Received information that the 1st Battn. K. R. Rifles had evacuated their position and that the enemy was advancing on the right. We sent out our heavily under Captain MILLER. Heavy fire which was concentrated on our sector and the position became untenable. Captain MILLER, therefore, gave the order to withdraw and reform behind its ridge in front of ARVILLERS. This withdrawal took place under a heavy artillery barrage. The fortnight of the party was now only about 40. Along with details of 1st and 2nd Rifles they dug in South of ARVILLERS. The enemy did not press his advance in this direction but seemed south towards GUERBIGNY.	
		4 p.m.	Received orders from 107th Brigade who were in position South of HANGEST that all details were to proceed there. When we had marched about ½ mile west of ARVILLERS, we met the G.O.C. 60th Brigade	

Atkinson Lieut.
for O.C. 15th Bn. Royal Irish Rifles

Army Form C. 2118.

15th Bn Royal Irish Rifles

WAR DIARY

INTELLIGENCE SUMMARY.

(Erase heading not required.)

Instructions regarding War Diaries and Intelligence Summaries are contained in F. S. Regs., Part II. and the Staff Manual respectively. Title pages will be prepared in manuscript.

Place	1918 Date March	Hour	Summary of Events and Information	Remarks and references to Appendices
	28	6 p.m.	who ordered us to hold a line of trenches running South from HANGEST – ARVILLERS road at that spot. In position and manned then throughout the night. Two and out patrols to the South every two hours but no enemy were seen or heard.	
			Between 8 a.m. and 10 a.m. the area was heavily shelled but no casualties were caused.	
		10.30 a.m	Received orders to withdraw to SOURDON as the 7o.th Brigade had been relieved by French troops	
SOURDON		7 pm	Arrived at SOURDON. Remained the night in this village	
VELENNES	29/30			
SALEUX	30/31		Spent the night at Railway Station	
MAIGNEVILLE	31		Arrived here. It is expected that the troops will have an opportunity for a good rest.	

A Minton Anderson
Lieut + Adjt
for O.C. 15th Bn. R.I. Rifles

1 07th Brigade.

36th Division.

1/15th BATTALION

ROYAL IRISH RIFLES

APRIL 1918.

Maps: Belgium
28. N.W.
Edition 6.

WAR DIARY 107 15th Battn
or R. Irish Rifle.
INTELLIGENCE SUMMARY 36
(Erase heading not required.)

Army Form C. 2118.

April 1918

Place	Date	Hour	Summary of Events and Information	Remarks and references to Appendices
	1	1 p.m.	The Battalion entrain at Solenc S¹ AMIENS at 9 a.m. Detrain at GAMACHES at 1 p.m. March from GAMACHES to MAIGNEVILLE where battalion is billeted	CWS
	2		At MAIGNEVILLE Drafts of 3 officers + 120 men from the 23rd Entrenching Batt. and 3 officers + 340 men from 21st Entrenching Batt join the Battalion. Major McCallum D.S.O. 21st Entrenching Batt assumes command of the Battalion vice Capt P.W. Mills M.C.	CWS
	3	10.30 p.m.	At Maigneville. The Battalion march to entraining station at 7.30 p.m. Arrived Feuquiers at 10.30 p.m.	CWS
	4	2 a.m.	Batt entrain at FEUQUIERES at 2 a.m. Arrive at PROVEN at 5 a.m. + proceed by bus to HOSPITAL FARM CAMP near ELVERDINGHE. Capt J.J. Hill M.C. appointed temporary adjutant.	CWS
	5		At HOSPITAL FARM. Paraded proceed to the line to reinforce trenches held by 1st Division under Major D McCallum D.S.O	CWS
	6		At HOSPITAL FARM. Battalion relieved front of 3rd (?) Brigade in line. Major Lepper M.C. rejoined the Battalion.	CWS
	7		In line Capt G.W. Sturnge M.C. assumes the duties of adjutant vice Capt J.J. Hill M.C. who returned his duties as Quartermaster.	CWS

WAR DIARY

INTELLIGENCE SUMMARY

(Erase heading not required.)

Army Form C. 2118.

Place	Date	Hour	Summary of Events and Information	Remarks and references to Appendices.
	April 8.		In the line. Situation Quiet. Weather fine	cubs
	9.		In the line. The Battalion is relieved by parts of 1st & 2nd Bns the Royal Irish Rifles. Battalion withdrew into Brigade Support North Battalion at Hengel Hulleart.	cubs
	10.		In Brigade Support. Replacements officers reinforcements	cubs
	11.		Lt. Col. R.D.P. MAXWELL D.S.O. took over command of the battalion.	cubs
	12.		Brigade support.	cubs
	13.		Battalion moved back into Brigade reserve at JOFFRE CAMP. C.19.d.9.7. being relieved by the 9th R. Innis. Fus. Ground reconnoitred for a new support line to be made away from KEMPTON PARK C.15.b.40.60 along ADMIRALS ROAD to BUFF. Rd C.22.b.60.80	cubs
	14.		Work on new support line.	cubs
	15.		do.	cubs
	16.		Battalion moved up to live in new support line. Battalion HQ being at FOCH F.M. C.20.d.10.85.	cubs

: − 3 −

WAR DIARY
INTELLIGENCE SUMMARY
(Erase heading not required.)

Army Form C. 2118.

Place	Date	Hour	Summary of Events and Information	Remarks and references to Appendices
	April 17		In Brigade Support. Work carried on on Support Line	C.R.L.S.
	18		do	C.R.L.S.
	19/20		Battalion relieved the 1st ROYAL IRISH RIFLES in the Line, our front running along the STEENBECK. Battalion H.Q. in huts at C.22.b.70.78.near MOUSE TRAP FM	C.R.L.S.
	20		In the Line.	C.R.L.S.
	21		do	C.R.L.S.
	22/23		Battalion was relieved by 2nd R. IRISH RIFLES in the line and withdrew into support with Bn. H.Q. at FOCH FARM	C.R.L.S.
	23		Bn. was relieved by 1st ROYAL IRISH RIFLES and withdrew to SIEGE CAMP into Brigade Reserve.	C.R.L.S.
	24		In Brigade Reserve.	C.R.L.S.

WAR DIARY

Army Form C. 2118.

(Erase heading not required.)

Place	Date	Hour	Summary of Events and Information	Remarks and references to Appendices
	April 25.		Lt. Col. R.D.P. MAXWELL, D.S.O. proceed to LONDON under instructions to report to War office, and was struck off strength of Battn. Lt. Col. R.C. SMYTHE, D.S.O. R. INNIS. FUS. took over command of Bn Battn.	AAA.
	26.		Battalion moved up to CANAL BANK in its Brigade support.	AAA
	27		do	AAA
	28		do	AAA
	29		do	AAA
	30		do	AAA

R.C. Smythe. Lieut. Col.
Comdg. 1st R. IRISH RIFLES

WAR DIARY
INTELLIGENCE SUMMARY
(Erase heading not required.)

15th R. Irish Rifles   Army Form C. 2118.

Vol 32

Place	Date	Hour	Summary of Events and Information	Remarks and references to Appendices
MAP REF. Sht 28 NW 1:20,000 BELGIUM	May 1st 1918.		Weather fine & warm & hot. Capt. P.M. MILLER M.C. to ENGLAND. Battalion relieved 2nd R. IRISH RIFLES in the line MOUSETRAP FARM sector (ST. JULIEN) without incident. "A" Coy Right forward Coy, "B" Coy Left forward Coy, "C" Coy counter-attack by "D" Coy Right support. "A" Coy 2nd R. IR. RIFLES Left Support. The 9th R. INNIS. FUSILIERS were on our right and the 18th R. L. LIENE (BELGIQUE) on our left. Some irregular shelling during the day. 2nd Lt. CRAWFORD wounded and 2 O.Rks. (gassed.) LT. J. IRELAND M.C. assumed command of "A" Coy.	
	2-5-18		Artillery fairly active on both sides. We pushed forward two posts. 1 O.R. killed by sniper.	
	3-5-18		Weather still fine. Continued promiscuous shelling by the enemy, our artillery active. We established new outpost.	
	4-5-18		Artillery active on both sides. Enemy attempted direct hit on "C" Coy Hqrs. HAMPSHIRE FARM and hit a small ammunition and very light dump near B. Coys. HQ. CAPT. F.S. WOODLEY M.C. wounded by shell fire.	
	5/5/18		At 3 a.m. our post at C.7 (C.17 "A" Coy) took a prisoner of 4/84th L.I.R. (1st LANDWEHR DIV.) Prisoner was unarmed and carrying a camp kettle. He stated that he had only joined his unit that day and told nothing of military importance. Wind changed from NE to SE and gave enemy Enemy artillery less active. Battalion on out nights.	

Army Form C. 2118.

WAR DIARY
INTELLIGENCE SUMMARY
(Erase heading not required.)

Place	Date	Hour	Summary of Events and Information	Remarks and references to Appendices
MARIE F. BELGIUM SHEET. 28 N.W. 1:20000	5/5/18 (cont)		The 9th R.INNIS.FUSILIERS were relieved by 2nd R.INNIS.FUSILIERS on night of 5/6th. Our casualties:- 2 O.Rks wounded by shell fire.	
	6/5/18		Rain early in the morning fine afternoon. At 4.30 a.m. our outpost at C.17.C.1.7. (A.Coy) took a prisoner of 184th L.I.R. (1st LANDWEHR DIV). Prisoner was unarmed. He stated that his battalion had relieved 484th L.I.R on night of 5/6th and were doing 3 days in the line. Enemy heavily shelled us during the evening. Battalion was relieved by 2nd R.I.R. night of 6/7th. Our outpost at C.17.C.1.7. took two above prisoners before midnight. One was a Sgt. Major, they seemed to 184th L.I.R. were armed and were rushed by two of A. Coy with fixed bayonets. Casualties 4 O.R.s M.McILVEEN.D.C.M and 1 O.Rk killed and 4 O.Rks wounded. Bell caused by enemy shell fire.	
	7/5/18		Battalion were relieved by 2nd R.I. RIFLES and proceeded to WAGRAM FARM and SOULT CAMP. 100 in our billets by 3 a.m. Rain during early morning fine afterwards. "B" & "D" Coys held trenches in Brigade Reserve. "A" & "C" Coys billeted in huts in SOULT CAMP. Day devoted to cleaning etc.	
	8/5/18		Enemy threw a lot of shrapnel around the camp, early in the morning:- One man killed and 3 men wounded. Work:- "A","C", & "D" Coys deepened the trenches at WAGRAM	

WAR DIARY or INTELLIGENCE SUMMARY

Army Form C. 2118.

MAP REF. BELGIUM Sheet 28 NW 1:20000

Place	Date	Hour	Summary of Events and Information	Remarks and references to Appendices
	8/5/18 (cont)		FARM under R.E. supervision. "B" Coy training. Weather fine and hot.	
	9/5/18		Enemy Trench M.G.s were very active during the early hours of the morning, but we suffered no casualties. Weather fine and hot. "B" & "D" Coys working on trenches. "A" Coy training. A Coy relieved a Coy of the 1st R.INNIS. FUSILIERS at HILL TOP FARM in the evening and came under O.C. 2nd R.I.RIFLES. Casualties nil.	
	10/5/18		Weather again hot. "B" & "D" Coys working on trenches. "C" Coy training. In the evening 1 Batt. H.Q. and 2 & "D" Coys relieved the 2nd R.INNIS. FUSILIERS in CANAL BANK EAST. "C" Coy Bde Reserve. "D" Coy in strongpoints before garrison from Belgians on left. "B" Coy relieved B Coy 2nd R.INNIS FUS. 2/8 IRISH FARM to No. 3 Bridge on right. B.Coy came under O.C. 1st R.I.RIFLES. Casualties Nil.	
	11/5/18		Weather hot and fine. Day quiet. In the evening we relieved the 2nd R.IRIFLES in the MOUSETRAP FARM sector. "A" Coy support "B" Coy number attack "C" Coy left front "D" Coy right front. 18th R.I. LIGNE (BELGIAN) on our left. 1st R.I.RIFLES on the right. Casualties nil. 1 Mr.	
	12/5/18		Day very misty until 1 pm after which it became overcast and full use was made of it by all sides with fatiguer and other reconnaissances. A patrol (strength 1 corporal 4 men) under Lieut. S. ARTREANOR (O.C. "B" Coy) went to for starvation during the following day.	

MAP REF. BELGIUM.
SHEET 28 NW & SW.

WAR DIARY
INTELLIGENCE SUMMARY
(Erase heading not required.)

Army Form C. 2118.

Place	Date	Hour	Summary of Events and Information	Remarks and references to Appendices
	12/5/18 (cont)		Hospital and Lieut H.C. MORROW, M.C. assumed command of "B" Coy. Enemy artillery quiet. Casualties 1 O.R. wounded.	
	13/5/18		Patrols left & scouts out in No Man's Land for observation during the day. They observed of the enemy leaving night posts and entering them. Day was fine but tended to storm in the evening. Hostile artillery quiet. One of our planes dropped a bomb near HILL TOP. Sk 5.45 p.m. a nile night post established by Right Coy H.Q. The Coy. Commanders of 1st R.I. Fus. came up to look round the area. Casualties. Nil.	Aug 13-A M.C. App 13 App 13/5
	14/5/18		Daytime shoot. Hostile artillery quiet, but shelled CANAL BANK twenty about 11.45 a.m. Very slow enemy with great irregularity on both sides. An enemy battery of field guns in the open spotted at APPLE VILLA. Aeroplane work and cross flag was flying. 30 O.R. left and Intelligence officer of 1st R.I. Fus. raided us. Lieut L.S. DUNCAN M.C. joined Battalion and assumed command of "D" Coy vice Lt. W.J. MORRISON: casualties Nil.	App
	15/5/18		6 patrols left & scouts on to trench hands for daylight observation. They observed 2 of the enemy at daybreak but were not sure if a post were held there. Day fine and hot. At 11.20 a.m. a French plane was brought down in NO MAN'S LAND. The aviator	

Army Form C. 2118.

MAP REF: BELGIUM.
Sht 28 NW 1:20000.

WAR DIARY
INTELLIGENCE SUMMARY.
(Erase heading not required.)

Place	Date	Hour	Summary of Events and Information	Remarks and references to Appendices
	15/5/18 (cont)		wounded through the leg, succeeded in reaching one of our outposts and came into our lines at dusk. He was an American. The enemy shelled the plane soon after it landed and obtained two or three direct hits on it. Some officers of the 1st R.I.F.Us. went round the place. Hostile artillery quiet. Casualties: Nil.	
	16/5/18		At 1 A.M. some of the gas from our gas shell bombardments apparently blew back over our lines. Trench mortar gas was also noticed, about the same hour. Day fine and hot. Enemy shelled BUFFS ROAD near HILLTOP FARM nearly from 10 A.M. to 12 noon. Some of the 1st R.I.F.Us. came in and remained with us until the relief on the following day.	
	17/5/18		Rally fine and hot. Enemy artillery fairly quiet. Aircraft very active. One of our planes was brought down in flames by a Bosche plane at 5.00 P.M. E of YPRES. Bosche plane brought down in flames near KITCHENERS WOOD during the morning. In the evening the 108th Bde. relieved 107th Bde, the 1st R.I.F.Us. relieved us after relief we marched to HOSPITAL FARM AREA. Bn. HQ at B.26.d.2.5. "A" & "B" Coy at WELSH FM. "C" Coy at B.26.d.7.5. "D" Coy on road in B.20.a. Casualties: Nil.	

Army Form C. 2118.

WAR DIARY
or
INTELLIGENCE SUMMARY.
(Erase heading not required.)

Place: MAP REF. BELGIUM SHEET 28. N.W. 1:20000.

Instructions regarding War Diaries and Intelligence Summaries are contained in F.S. Regs., Part II. and the Staff Manual respectively. Title pages will be prepared in manuscript.

Date	Hour	Summary of Events and Information	Remarks and references to Appendices
18/5/18		Day very warm. Rested & cleaning up. Capt. C.N.L. STRONGE. M.C. (2nd R. INNIS. FUS) att. as Adjutant proceeded to hospital. Lieut A.N. ANDERSON took over the duties of Adjutant.	
19/5/18		Weather dry and very warm. Battalion attended Church Services. Great artillery activity at DICKEBUSH during the night.	
20/5/18		Fine and hot. Coys worked on the "GREEN LINE" from 9 a.m. to 3.30 p.m. Lt. F.S. TOOLEY. M.C. joined for duty and assumed command of "B" Coy vice Lieut. H.G. MORROW M.C.	
21/5/18		Exceedingly warm. Coys. worked on the "GREEN LINE" from 6 a.m. – 12 noon.	
22/5/18		Fine and hot. Lt. Col. R.C. SMYTHE. D.S.O. proceeded to G.H.Q. to visit various Schools of Instruction. Major J.D.M. McCALLUM. D.S.O. assumed temporary command. Day devoted to training. The A.D.M.S. gave a lecture on "SANITATION". In the evening the talented members of the Battalion gave a very enjoyable concert.	
23/5/18		Fine and hot. Coys. worked on the "GREEN LINE" from 6 a.m. to 12 noon. O.C. 'A' Coy. Lieut J. IRELAND M.C. went to hospital. Lieut. H.G. MORROW M.C. resumed command of 'A' Coy.	

WAR DIARY
INTELLIGENCE SUMMARY.

Army Form C. 2118.

Place	Date	Hour	Summary of Events and Information	Remarks and references to Appendices
MAP REF. BELGIUM SHEET 28 N.W. 1:20,000	24/5/18		Day cooler and wet. Work on "GREEN LINE" cancelled for the day. Companies training in billets. Football match the Battalion played at arms of the 16th Div Royal Irish Rifles at "Somme Camp" was drawn 1–1 nil.	N/m
	25/5/18		Weather fine. Companies training section drill, and platoon drill. Lt. Col. R.C. SMYTHE. D.S.O., returned and assumed command.	N/m
	26/5/18		Weather fine and hot. Church Parades.	N/m
	27/5/18		Weather fine and hot. Companies working on "GREEN LINE".	N/m
	28/5/18		Fine. Capt. A.J.P. THORNTON. M.C., took over the duties of Adjutant vice Lieut. A.N. ANDERSON, who assumed the duties of Asst. Adjutant. Companies working on GREEN LINE. Battalion bathing at ROBAL BATHS. Football match the battalion played a team of the II Corps Tenthy. Works Battn. at "SOMME CAMP" and won 2 to 1. I.E.A. brought down 5 of our Observation Balloons in flames. 107th Bde. relieved the 108th Bde. on night of 29/30th. We relieved the 1st R. IRISH FUSILIERS in MOUSETRAP sector. The 2nd Bn R.I. RIFLES on Right and the 2nd Battn. 7 K.P. de LIGNE (Belgian) on our left. Dispositions of Battn. – "A" Coy Right FRONT, B Coy Left FRONT, C Coy Counter-Attack Coy. D Coy Support Coy. Lt. A.H. ALLEN joined and was posted to "B" Coy. 2nd Lt. T.B. STEPHENSON. M.C. joined and was posted to "A" Coy. 2nd Lt. J. McLARNON perished and was posted to "A" Coy. Casualties :- 4 ORks killed and 10RK wounded by shell fire whilst coming into the line	N/m

Army Form C. 2118.

WAR DIARY
INTELLIGENCE SUMMARY.
(Erase heading not required.)

Instructions regarding War Diaries and Intelligence Summaries are contained in F. S. Regs., Part II. and the Staff Manual respectively. Title pages will be prepared in manuscript.

Place	Date	Hour	Summary of Events and Information	Remarks and references to Appendices
MAP. REF. BELGIUM Sheet 28.N.W. 1:20000	30/5/18		Day fine. 2/Lt. J. KNOX. M.C. returned from hospital. Enemy artillery quiet. Great aerial activity. 1 E.A. brought down near WIELTJE during morning, and one of our planes crashed during the evening, also near WIELTJE. Casualties ✠ 2 O.Rks Killed, 1 O.Rk Wounded by shell fire.	M/n
	31/5/18		Fine and very warm. Enemy quiet. Much aerial activity on both sides. Lt. Col. R.C. SMYTHE. D.S.O. admitted to hospital. Major J.D.M. M^cCALLUM assumed command of Battalion. Casualties:- 1 O.Rk Wounded at duty shell fire. 1 O.Rk Wounded by M.G. fire. Locality the Battalion occupied a keen at the 1st Battery Belgian Horse Artillery at Wieltje + arm S. to 1.	N/n

In the Field
1/6/18

[signature]
Major
Commdg. 15th(S) Bn. Royal Irish Rifles.

WAR DIARY
INTELLIGENCE SUMMARY

Army Form C. 2118.

15th Bn. R. Irish Rifles

Place	Date	Hour	Summary of Events and Information	Remarks and references to Appendices
MAP REF BELGIUM Sheet 28 NW 5/2W.W.C.	1/8/18		Fine & hot. Colonel and four officers of the 19th Manchesters (Belgian) visited us to reconnoitre our sub-sector. Relieved on night of 1/2nd by 2nd R. IR. RIF. and after relief went into CANAL BANK. Batt. Hqrs. A & B Coys. in CANAL BANK. C Coy. just N. of BURNT FARM. D. Coy. at BURNT FARM. Casualties :- Nil	A/m
	2/8/18		Fine but much cooler. Coys providing various working parties forward of the CANAL and in the line. Capt. C.N.L. STRONGE M.C. returns from hospital. Casualties :- Nil	A/m
	3/8/18		Fine. Lt. J. IRELAND M.C., returns from hospital. 2 Lt. J.S. McLARNON to hospital. Working parties as usual. Casualties :- Nil	A/m
	4/8/18		Fine. Working parties as usual. 2nd Lt. T.B. STEPHENSON M.C., attached temporarily to 2nd R.IR. RIF. Advance parties of BELGIANS reported to Batt. Hqrs. Casualties Nil.	A/m
	5/8/18		Fine & hot. Sub-sector relieved by 6th Bn. (Belgian) on night of 5/6th. Battalion relieved by 6 Coys. 1st Grenadiers. 2 Coys. 4th Carabiniers. After relief, the Battn. moved to ROAD CAMP. Shell 27, E25, d.2.3. Entraining at READING detraining at KORTEK. Battn. all in camp by 6 a.m. Casualties 1 OR wounded, 1 OR accidentally wounded.	A/m
ROAD CAMP Sheet 27 E.25.d.2.3.	6/8/18		Day fine. Devoted to cleaning. American gas officer inspected the Box Respirator.	A/m
	7/8/18		Fine & hot. Day devoted to interior economy and re-organisation. LT. SCOTT R.A.M.C. to hospital. Re-turns at R.R.M.C. CAMP Bath.	A/m

Army Form C. 2118.

WAR DIARY
or
INTELLIGENCE SUMMARY.
(Erase heading not required.)

Instructions regarding War Diaries and Intelligence Summaries are contained in F. S. Regs., Part II. and the Staff Manual respectively. Title pages will be prepared in manuscript.

Place	Date	Hour	Summary of Events and Information	Remarks and references to Appendices
ROAD CAMP BELGIUM Sheet 27 B.5.d.2.3.	8/9/18		2nd. Lieut. A. MOSBY M.O.R.C. U.S.A. from 109th F.A. as Medical Officer. A party of Officers & N.C.Os reconnoitred the BLUE LINE, the tracks leading up to it, and from it to the YELLOW LINE. This party was taken to 'P' Camp by bus. Bathing at ROAD CAMP Baths. Coys reorganizing etc.	
"	9/9/18		Fine. Church Parades.	
"	10/9/18		Lt.Col. R.C. SMYTHE, D.S.O., returns from hospital. Capt. W.R. LANGTRY and 2nd Lt. W. LINTON arrive and posted to "C" Coy. Released by Corps Commanders instruction killed by the Brig General in the morning. Afternoon was very wet and the parade was dismissed before the Corps Commander arrived. The General Sir C. JACOB K.C.B. talked to all Officers of 107 Bde.	
"	11/9/18		Fine. Coys training. The Corps Commander visited the batln during the Evening. Runner Amount instructed the rifles.	
"	12/9/18		Fine. Coys training. Capt N.R. LANGTRY & 2nd Lt. C.E. BEATTY to hospital. Transports Competition judged by Brig General E.V. THORPE D.S.O. who wished his congratulations to be conveyed to the winners.	

(A7092) Wt. W12539/M1293. 75,000. 1/17. D. D. & L., Ltd. Forms/C.2118/14.

WAR DIARY or INTELLIGENCE SUMMARY

Army Form C. 2118.

Place	Date	Hour	Summary of Events and Information	Remarks and references to Appendices
PENTON CAMP	13/8/18		Battalion moved to PENTON CAMP (PROVEN) and changed over with 1st R.IR.RIF. Coy. moved off from ROAD CAMP at 2.45 am and 3.15 am. Arrived at ROUTE K and entrained at MISSION Jn (A+B) WESTONHOEK (C+D) to work on VLAMERTINGHE LINE and E. POPERINGHE LINE indentically. Coys returned to PENTON CAMP after work, work started at 1.30 pm. Travelling by rail to PUGWASH.	
"	14/8/18		Lt. Col. R.C. SMYTHE D.S.O. proceeded on leave to ENGLAND. Major J.D.M. M°CALLUM D.S.O. assumed command. Coys. working as before, except that they entrained at PUGWASH. The C.O. inspected the Officers and Battn. Headquarters Coys. working in usual whilst C+D Coys were returning by light railway a train on broad gauge ran into them. 4 ORKS were killed and 14 Other ranks injured. The battn cricket team played the 110th F.A. at ROUSBRUGGE and won by 63 runs to 50. LT. J. SCOTT R.A.M.C. returned from hospital.	
"	15/8/18		Inf. Church Parades. Battalion sports in afternoon at flying ground PROVEN. Result:- 1. SCHOOL (CLASSES) 16 pts, 2. TRANSPORT + "C" Coy 15½ pts ea, 3. "B" Coy 13 pts, 4. "A" Coy 9 pts, 5. Battn HQ 5 pts. 6. "D" Coy, 3 pts. Brig General E.K. THORPE D.S.O., attended the sports meeting.	

Army Form C. 2118.

WAR DIARY
INTELLIGENCE SUMMARY.
(Erase heading not required.)

Place	Date	Hour	Summary of Events and Information	Remarks and references to Appendices
PENTON CAMP PROVEN	17/9/18		All Coys working in Reserved Sector of ESPERINGHE huts, proceeding and returning by train as before. Lt. H P MOSBY M.O.R.C. U.S.A. appointed M.O. to the Battn. vice Lt. T.E.SCOTT R.A.M.C to 109th F.A. 2nd Lt R.K.ROBINSON "B"Coy finished 4th in the Hill Open at the 36.4 Bore Coy & Platoon Shoots	MN
"	18/9/18		All coys working as previous day. Party reconnoitring Battn. sector in ESPERINGHE huts and the approaches thereto. 1hr wounded by splinters from AA shell. Casualties – 1hr wounded by splinters from AA shell.	MN
"	19/9/18		Coys working as previous day. The Battn. football team beat the 2nd R.I.R.T.I.F. 7 goals to nil	MN
"	20/9/18		Coys working as previous day. Advance party of the 9th R INNIS. FUS. reconnoitring them. The Battn. Cricket team played the 9 Innis Fus. Team (A.S.C.) match was abandoned unfinished owing to rain. Score Our Team 61 all out Battn. 17 for 1 wicket	MN
TUNNELLERS CAMP	21/9/18		The Battalion moved to TUNNELLERS CAMP taking over the billets occupied by the 9th R. INNIS. FUSILIERS. The battalion team played the Divisional HQrs cricket team and won by 94 runs to 61.	MN
"	22/9/18		Parades under Company arrangements	MN
"	23/9/18		Church Parade. The battalion football team beat the 109th F.A. 3 goals to nil.	MN

WAR DIARY
INTELLIGENCE SUMMARY.
(Erase heading not required.)

Army Form C. 2118.

Place	Date	Hour	Summary of Events and Information	Remarks and references to Appendices
TUNNELLERS CAMP.	24/6/18		"A" Coy. on range at TUNNELLERS CAMP. Remainder doing company and platoon training. The battalion cricket team played the Divisional Train (A.S.C.) and were beaten by 107 runs to 89.	
	25/6/18		"B" Coy. and H.Qrs. on PROVEN AERODROME at company and Platoon Training. Remainder at Batt'n training on the football ground TUNNELLERS CAMP. The battalion cricket team played the 147 Battery R.G.A and won by 90 runs to 39. Sports- Standard tests.	
	26/6/18		"B" Coy. on range. "A", "C", & "D" Coys platoon and company training. The Divisional Gas Officer tested the Batt'ns box respirators. The battalion football team beat the 56th Div. Train (A.S.C.) 4 goals to nil. Sports - standard tests.	
	27/6/18		"C" Coy. on the range. "A", "B", & "D" Coys platoon and company training. The battalion cricket team played the 351st Siege R.G.A and were beaten by 131 runs to 47. Sports - Standard tests.	
	28/6/18		"A" & "D" Coys. at PROVEN aerodrome carrying out small scheme. "B" & "C" Coys. platoon and coy. training. Div. HQrs beat the battalion cricket team by 124 runs to 104. Sports- Standard tests.	
	29/6/18		8 a.m - 10.30 a.m. "D" Coy. on range. "A", "B", and "C" Coys. Platoon and company training. 11.15am Battalion Parade. Brig.General E.N. THORPE. D.S.O. presented medal ribbons to Offrs and O.Rks. The battn football team beat the 153 Bde. R.G.A by 6 goals to nil.	

Army Form C. 2118.

WAR DIARY
INTELLIGENCE SUMMARY.
(Erase heading not required.)

Place	Date	Hour	Summary of Events and Information	Remarks and references to Appendices
TUNNELLERS CAMP.	30/1/18		Church Parades. Party recorded the Battalion sector of the BLUE LINE. The Battalion football team beat the 1st R. IRISH RIFLES in regards to kit. A Battalion memorial service (1st July) was held, the service was conducted by Capt. Hutchinson C.F. and Capt. R. Watson C.F.	

J. Mulholland
Major
Commdg. 15th (S) Bn. R. Irish Rifles

WAR DIARY
INTELLIGENCE SUMMARY
(Erase heading not required.)

Army Form C. 2118.

15th R. Irish Rifles

Vol 34

Place	Date	Hour	Summary of Events and Information	Remarks and references to Appendices
Sercus Camp.	1 July 1918		Divisional Horse Show. Battalion obtained 1st in "Mule Race" + 3rd in "Limbers & Light Draught" Competition.	
do	2 "		Companies training. "A" & "D" at PROVEN AERODROME "B" & "C" TUNNELLERS CAMP. 1 Officer & 1 N.C.O. billeting to ST. SYLVESTRE CAPPEL.	
ST SYLVESTRE CAPPEL	3 "		Battalion marched to new billets in ST. SYLVESTRE CAPPEL. Foot inspection in afternoon by M.O. C.O. & 4 other officers reconnoitred Battalion Sector of Reserve Line at MT. DES CATS.	
do	4 "		Baths at CASSEL. Companies Kit Inspection. Lt. Col. R.C. Smythe D.S.O. returned from leave. Football Match. Battalion v. 210 Squadron R.A.F. O.	
do	5 "		Baths at CASSEL. Companies training. Advance party to reconnoitre positions held by Reserve Bathn. & Front Line Battn. of 128th Infantry Regt. (French) Party to remain in line until Battn. arrives on night of 6/7th inst.	
do	6 "		Battalion moved from ST. SYLVESTRE CAPPEL to MT des CATS, moving off at 4p.m. & relieved the 2nd Bn. of 128th French Infantry Battn. Relief complete 2 am.	
MT des CATS	7 "		Battalion moved from MT des CATS at 10.30 p.m. to Front Line, relieving the Battn. of 128th French Infantry Regt. Relief complete at 3 am. R.C. Smythe Lt. Colonel Commanding 15th (S) Bn. The R.I. Rifles.	

Army Form C. 2118.

WAR DIARY
INTELLIGENCE SUMMARY.
(Erase heading not required.)

Place	Date	Hour	Summary of Events and Information	Remarks and references to Appendices
FRONT LINE	8 July.		Everything was quiet during the day, but at night Artillery & M.G's were more active. One plane flew over our lines just before dawn but was driven back by our Lewis Gunners. At about 9 p.m. a slight bombardment was heard on our right. 2/Lt. W.J. Mercer proceeded to the R.A.F. England.	
do	9 "		Our artillery was very active all day, but the enemy only sent over about 10 heavy shrapnel shells. Several "Crumps" dropped near Benedict X Roads about 3 p.m. About 9 p.m. two pigeons flew in a line from Bethn. H.A. towards BAILLEUL.	
do	10 "		We had 2 daylight patrols out & one of them gained some good information about the enemy. Casualties 3 O.R. wounded.	
do	11 "		The day was very quiet again as usual, but at night artillery & M.G's fairly active. The enemy's aircraft was very active today. We have been improving the farm HQrs. are living in, & already a great improvement is noticeable. Heavy rain all last night & a lot during the day.	
do	12 "		We found to our disadvantage during the night that the farm leaked. There was very intense firing on our right & partly on our own	R.E. Anystette [?] Command 15th (S) Bn The R.I. Reg.

1577 Wt. W10791/1773 500,000 1/15 D.D.&L. A.D.S.S./Forms/C. 2118.

WAR DIARY

INTELLIGENCE SUMMARY.

(Erase heading not required.)

Army Form C. 2118.

Place	Date	Hour	Summary of Events and Information	Remarks and references to Appendices
Line	12 July		Front behind front line & round HQrs of our Right Coy. During the day everything was very quiet. A lot of Golden Rain lights were put up tonight.	
do.	13 "		Everything was as usual today except for the Artillery. Enemy's Artillery got a few shots near HQrs.	
do	14 "		Artillery was active again today. Pigeons were observed flying over our lines towards the enemy from direction of MT DES CATS to BAILLEUL.	
do	15 "		Artillery active & very slight Machine Gun fire. Patrols as usual. Casualties. 1.O.R. wounded.	
Reserve	16 "		Artillery active. No movement was observed during the day. We came out of the line into reserve on the night 15/16.	
do	17 "		Capt L.S. Tooley M.C. left us today to join the Flying Corps. Lt. R.S. Morrow M.C. took command of his (B) Coy. Capt. Laughy left also to go as Area Commandant. Casualties 2 O.R. wounded.	
do	18 "		Working parties were supplied tonight from all Companies for work	

R.E. Smythe
Commanding 13th (S) Bn the R.I. Rif

WAR DIARY
INTELLIGENCE SUMMARY
(Erase heading not required.)

Army Form C. 2118.

Place	Date	Hour	Summary of Events and Information	Remarks and references to Appendices
Reserve	18 July		on the BLUE LINE.	
"	19 "		Working parties again tonight. Inter Company relief.	
"	20 "		2/Lt. L. Money Left us today to join the Machine Gun Corps, Grantham.	
			Working parties as usual.	
"	21 "		Lt. Knuffer joined the Battalion today & was posted to B Coy, also 2/Lt.	
			P. Kelly, posted to D Coy. Working parties as usual.	
"	22 "		Lt. R. Smyth joined Battalion & was posted to C. Coy. Working parties	
			as usual.	
"	23 "		Working parties as usual. Tonight there was a Battalion relief	
			& we moved into Support & relieved the 2nd Batt. who moved into	
			Front line. Casualties 1 O.R. Killed, 2 O.R. wounded.	
Support	24 "		Companies at work improving their Billets & Positions.	
"	25 "		Companies working. Working parties on Support Line at night.	
"	26 "		Companies bathing. Enemy shelling very active. Louvacq 1 O.R. wounded.	
"	27 "		Working parties on Support Line at night. Enemy Artillery active.	
"	28 "		Working parties on Support Line at night. D. Morin left the Batt. today	

WAR DIARY
INTELLIGENCE SUMMARY
(Erase heading not required.)

Army Form C. 2118.

Place	Date	Hour	Summary of Events and Information	Remarks and references to Appendices
Luffort	28 July		USR	
			4 Lt Johnson (new M.O.) took over duties	[illeg]
	29 "		A, B & C Coys working on Support line at night. Enemy shelling	[illeg]
			Casualties 1. O.R. wounded.	
	30 "		Companies working on Mills and Bullets & Pastures. Enemy Artillery	[illeg]
			Active. Casualties 1. OR killed. 3. O.R. wounded.	
	31 "		Battalion relieved the 2nd Bn. Royal Irish Rifles in the line.	[illeg]
			Weather fine.	

R. E. Smythe
Lt Colonel
Commdg 15th Bn Lo A.I.Rd.

Army Form C. 2118.

WAR DIARY
or
INTELLIGENCE SUMMARY.
(Erase heading not required.)

15th R. Irish Rifles

Instructions regarding War Diaries and Intelligence Summaries are contained in F.S. Regs. Part II. and the Staff Manual respectively. Title pages will be prepared in manuscript.

Place	Date	Hour	Summary of Events and Information	Remarks and references to Appendices
In the Line	1/8/18		Enemy's artillery was quiet during the day. Two patrols went out during the night.	
do.	2/8/18		Everything quiet. Casualties 1 O.R. wounded.	
do.	3/8/18		Enemy artillery more active today. 2/Lieut McCrea joined us today posted to 'B' Company.	
do.	4/8/18		Everything quiet - 2 patrols out during day. Wiring at night. Casualties 2 O.Rs killed	
do	5/8/18		Enemy artillery very active, Casualties 2 ORs killed	
do	6/8/18		Everything quiet. Patrols out day and night. Wiring &c. Casualties 1 O.R. wounded 2nd Lt J.R. McKenney + 2/Lt W. Anderson wounded	
do.	7/8/18		Situation normal — daylight patrols out — Casualties 2 O.R wounded.	
	8/8/18		Enemy aircraft more active, bombs dropped near X.S.A.	
			Relief — went to Div: Reserve - RIFLE RANGE WOOD (Bn H.Qrs)	
RESERVE.	9/8/18		Six 4.2s fell outside Bn HQrs - no working parties, except small parties to repair holes in road caused by shell fire — 1 O.R. wounded. RATHKENNY. O.P. established by scouts.	

W.N. Smyth Lee
Lieut.-Colonel.

WAR DIARY
or
INTELLIGENCE SUMMARY.

Army Form C. 2118.

Place	Date	Hour	Summary of Events and Information	Remarks and references to Appendices
RESERVE.	10/8/18		Artillery active - enemy low flying plane brought down - All Coys supplied working parties in BLUE LINE. - 1 O.R. wounded. 2 R.E.s wounded. Bn. H.Qrs lightly shelled.	WWB Lt. Col. R.L. Amyss D.S.O to B.E. H.Q. Temp. B.G. during leave absence of B. Gen E. Thorpe D.S.O
do.	11/8/18		Few H.E.s outside Bn HQrs. Lieut ELLIS & 2/Lt WEBB reported for duty.	WWB
do.	12/8/18	At 9.3 pm	Except for shelling in RIFLE RANGE WOOD - day quiet - enemy threw about 30 GAS shells in same locality - 2 casualties (slight). - 'B' Coy one platoon, on way up to work were GAS shelled - casualties 2 incl Lt McCrea and 4 other hands - (all slight). Major McCallum D.S.O arrived.	WWB
do.	13/8/18		Very quiet - SENLAC FARM. shelled - 2, 5.9s dropped immediately in rear of farm - Casualties 2 killed 4 wounded - 1 shell short. At 11.30 pm, working Large numbers of Gas shells thrown into R.34.d. - Several parties had to move to right to prevent casualties - Several slight cases of gas in Battalion.	WWB

R.C. Smyth
Lieut.-Colonel,
Commanding 13th (S) Battn. The Royal Irish Rifles

Army Form C. 2118.

WAR DIARY
or
INTELLIGENCE SUMMARY.
(Erase heading not required.)

Instructions regarding War Diaries and Intelligence Summaries are contained in F. S. Regs., Part II. and the Staff Manual respectively. Title pages will be prepared in manuscript.

Place	Date	Hour	Summary of Events and Information	Remarks and references to Appendices
RESERVE	14/8/18		Day very quiet - several men went down slightly gassed. 2/Lt IRONS and 2/Lt O.H.H. NUTTALL reported back from leave.	AWS
do	15/8/18		Rather heavy trial shelling.	AWS
do	16/9/18		Quiet during day. Bn: moved from RESERVE to FRONT LINE - good relief. 1 O.R. wounded.	AWS
FRONT LINE	17/8/18	3 A.M.	Our Artillery made a good shoot on wire WIRRAL FARM for 15 min - rather heavy retaliation. - 1 O.R. wounded.	AWS
do	18/8/18		Enemy shelling active - Operation on our right by 9th-7.29th Divisions, caused heavy retaliation on PELMAN, RISKY and KOPJE farms - also Front and Support lines from 11.30 to 2pm. Casualties 5 men wounded. Evening very quiet. Capt E.W.J. Stronge MC departed for leave. 2/Lt R. Young from Lewis Gun course.	AWS, Appx A
do	19/8/18		Heavy gas shelling in areas in R.15.c - X.H.D. and X.S.A from 3.0am to 4-30 am. - Patrol out at WIRRAL FARM from B Company at midnight to report on wire after artillery shoot. - Advance parties of 12th Rifles reported to take over. - Casualties - 2 O.R. killed 2 O.R. wounded	Appx B Appx 3.2

Lieut.-Colonel,
Commanding 15th (S) Battn., The Royal Irish Rifles

WAR DIARY
or
INTELLIGENCE SUMMARY.
(Erase heading not required.)

Army Form C. 2118.

Place	Date	Hour	Summary of Events and Information	Remarks and references to Appendices
FRONT LINE.	20th		Very little shelling – "B" Coy made an investigation on WIRRAL FARM one casualty 2/Lt E.L. Knight wounded (slight). – Front Line and Supports shelled 4-30 am – 5-30 am – Casualties 2 OR killed 2 OR wounded. 30th Divn advances line on our left.	AWS
do.	21st and 22nd		30th Divn advances line on our left and day quiet. – The Bn: Captured MURAL and WIRRAL FARMS – line advanced to a depth of 500 yds, most successful operation – Casualties 2/Lts (Officers and men) – 5 men killed 2 missing – 41 wounded. – 2/Lieuts STEPHENSON – NUTTALL – YOUNG wounded. – Three counter attacks beaten off at 6-30 pm – 10-30 pm and 11 pm with heavy loss to enemy. – Relieved at 11 pm by 12th Rifles – in middle of relief enemy counter attacked – heavy barrage – relief completed with few casualties. Three platoons 12th Rifles helped beat off counter attack. – Bn on being relieved went into Bde: Reserve –	AWS
RESERVE.	23rd		Bn. in Reserve – Battn in billets by 4 am – after over 45 days in trenches etc. – Operation by 108th Brigade successful R.D. Perceval-Price	AWS

Lt. Col.
Commanding 15th (S) Battn., The Royal Irish Rifles

Army Form C. 2118.

WAR DIARY
or
INTELLIGENCE SUMMARY.
(Erase heading not required.)

Instructions regarding War Diaries and Intelligence Summaries are contained in F. S. Regs., Part II. and the Staff Manual respectively. Title pages will be prepared in manuscript.

Place	Date	Hour	Summary of Events and Information	Remarks and references to Appendices
RESERVE	24th		Working parties — Capt. H. Morrow left for leave — also 2/Lt W.O. Leeper	
do.	25th		Working parties and baths — 2/Lt T. Knox left for leave — leave going steady — good things — Lieut J. Morrison reported from Army Course — Orders came in to be ready to move back for a rest. Lt. T. Stirling sent at ease as billeting officer — Companies bathing.	
	26th		Lieut C.D. Smythe left Battn. to rejoin 2nd LEINSTER REGT. 'C' Company had 4 casualties on working party 10 R Killed 3 O.R. wounded	
	27th		Weather broken, heavy rain. Battn. relieved — at Hdq. by 15th Bn. Cheshire Regt. in the BLUE LINE by 10th Bn. R. Scot Fusiliers, 31st Division — After relief battalion marched to Camp at Ref P.7 Central (Sheet 27) close to SYLVESTRE CAPPEL arriving there at 3.30 a.m. 28th Aug. Camp consists of tents and shelters	
	28th		Heavy showers stormy and much cooler. Battn. resting and cleaning up. Lt.Col R.C. SMYTH D.S.O. returned from Bde. and resumed command.	
	29th		Battalion resting. Fine day.	

T.E. Harding
Lieut.-Colonel,
Commanding 15th (S) Battn. The Royal Irish Rifles

Army Form C. 2118.

WAR DIARY
or
INTELLIGENCE SUMMARY.
(Erase heading not required.)

Instructions regarding War Diaries and Intelligence Summaries are contained in F. S. Regs., Part II. and the Staff Manual respectively. Title pages will be prepared in manuscript.

Place	Date	Hour	Summary of Events and Information	Remarks and references to Appendices
Ref. Contoul SHEET 27.	30th		Advancing Battalion paraded and the C.O. told them how much he appreciated the work they did in the operation on the 29th/30th inst. Companies engaged in Platoon training. Runs received that our troops had taken BAILLEUL.	Appx
	31st		This day Runs returned that 109 Bde had taken the KEMMELBERG RIDGE and that KEMMEL HILL had fallen. Orders arrived at 12.15 pm to move at 1 pm to MONT NOIR. Everyone hustled and the Batt. got away up to time. Billeted at MONT NOIR in various huts and sheds.	Appx

R. P. Smyth
Lieut.-Colonel,
Commanding 15th (S) Batt., The Royal Irish Rifles

SECRET   Copy No. 7

Battalion Operation Orders No. 21

1/ An inter-company relief will take place tomorrow night 4/5 Augt as follows:-
H Coy relieves C Coy   Right Front
B "   "   D "   Left "
On relief C Coy will withdraw into the area now occupied by H Coy & will become counter attack Coy.
D Coy will withdraw into the area now occupied by B Coy and will become Reserve Coy.

2/ Coys will take over the dispositions now in force in the Coys they relieve.
Trench Stores, working & carrying parties will be handed over.

3/ Completion of relief to be wired to Battn HQ in code using name of C.S.M.

4/ <u>ACKNOWLEDGE</u>

3/8/18   W.L.Shaye Cpt dsm
                                       J O D 1

FILE

SECRET.   Copy No..........

15th(S) Bn. The Royal Irish Rifles.
OPERATION ORDER No. 24.

1.   The Battalion will relieve the 1st Bn. Royal Irish Rifles in the Line on the night of the 16/17th August 1918.

2.   Companies will relieve as follows :-
         "C" Company to Right Front Line.
         "D"   "   " Left   "   "
         "A"   "   " Counter-attack.
         "B"   "   " Reserve.

3.   Companies to move off in the above order at midnight- 50 yds between platoons, and 200 yds. between Companies. "B" Company (Nucleous Garrison) will not move until relieved.

4. GUIDES.
         "B" and "A" Companies will not require guides. Guides for "C" and "D" Companies will be at KOPJE FARM (1 per platoon.)

5. ADVANCE PARTY.   An advance party of 1 Officer and 2 N.C.Os. per Company, will proceed to the Line to-night.

6.   The 12th Bn. Royal Irish Rifles will take over the present area occupied by this Battalion, if necessary Companies will leave small parties to hand over trench stores etc. to incoming Companies.

7.   All trench stores, special maps, aeroplane photos. etc., will be handed over and taken over and duplicate receipts forwarded to this office by 6-0 p.m. 17th inst.

8.   Completion of relief to be wired in code using name of Company Commander.

                    A C K N O W L E D G E.

                           (Sgd) C.N.L. STRONGE. Capt. & Adjt.
                           15th(S) Bn.The Royal Irish Rifles.

Copies to:-
107th Infantry Brigade.
Commanding Officer.
1st Bn. Royal Irish Rifles.
12th Bn. Royal Irish Rifles.
O.C., "A" Company.
O.C., "B"   "
O.C., "C"   "
O.C., "D"   "
Transport Officer.
Quartermaster.
Intelligence Officer.
R.S.M.
War Diary.
File.

Adjutant

War Diary

Copy No. 2

Operation Order No. 28

21/8/18.

Map issued herewith.

1. The Battalion will take and hold line shewn in red on attached map to-night.
   Zero hour will be communicated later.

2. **Dispositions.**
   "A" Company will capture MURAL FARM and RATION HOUSE and will consolidate RED LINE from X.17.a.50.32. - X.17.b.92.65. There will be two Platoons in the front covering area mentioned, with two platoons respectively about X.17.a.60.60. & X.17.b.40.95.
   "C" Company. will capture RED LINE and consolidate it from X.17.b.92.65 to X.12.c.70.35. (Road inclusive)
   There will be two Platoons in front, one Platoon in support about X.12.c.15.50 and one Platoon in Support in our old front line, about X.12.a.40.25.
   "B" Company. less two Platoons will capture and consolidate RED LINE from X.12.c.70.35 to about S.7.d.30.60. One Platoon in front with one Platoon in support about X.12.c.80.85. Remaining two Platoons "B" Company will capture WIRRAL FARM and consolidate Red line to S.8.a.05.40.

   The 1st Bn. The Royal Irish Rifles will establish a post about S.8.a.15.65 and will establish touch with our left post.
   "D" Company will occupy areas as mentioned on map issued herewith.

3. **BARRAGE.**
   (a) ZERO. Discharge of projectors by Special Coy. R.E.
   ZERO plus 1. Artillery barrage on line POE CROSS - X.18.a.20.35. - X.12.c.00.50.
   ZERO " 4. Barrage lifts to X.17.c.70.71 - X.18.a.10.10. - X.12.c.00.50.
   ZERO " 40. Enfilade Barrage moves E.50 per two minutes as far as grid line between squares X. and S.
   ZERO " 60. Enfilade Barrage ceases and comes down on line X.18.c.10.75. - S.13.b.45.65.
   ZERO " 85. Barrage ceases.
   (b) ZERO " 1 to) 6"Hows. bombard WIRRAL FARM
       ZERO " 10   )
       ZERO " 10 to) 6" Hows. cease and two 4.5 Hows. bombard
       ZERO " 20   ) WIRRAL FARM.
       ZERO " 20. Barrage ceases.
   (c) **MACHINE GUNS.** M.G. of Division on right will put down barrage S. of POE CROSS - APPETITE FARM ROAD and will be continued by our M.G's. from X.18.a.50.40 to S.13.b.00.30. They will also fire on roads from BAILLEUL.

4. **METHOD OF ATTACK.** O.C., Coys. will report when they are
   ASSEMBLY POSITIONS (See Map) in their position, by runner to Bn H.Q
   (a) "A" Company. 2 Platoons in INTERNATIONAL Trench X.17.a.50.60. 1 Platoon in ditch on road at X.71.c.48.25. Reserve Platoon will be in our front line trench about X.11.d.50.60. till ZERO plus 1. when they will move and occupy switch trench about S.11.c.70.20.
   Nos.1-2 Platoons will capture RATION HOUSE & MURAL FARM.
   No.3 Platoon will clear hedges X.17.b.10.45. - X.17.a.50.30 and gain touch with Division on right about X.17.a.50.30.
   No.4 Platoon will be in reserve under the O.C., Company, to help in case of severe opposition being encountered.
   No.1 Platoon will work along hedge to corner at X.17.b.10.60. and thence to X.17.b.20.83. Here party will divide ,(a) to go along hedge to X.17.b.55.35. and thence to X.11.d.55.16.,(b) will work along hedge from X.17.b.20.83. -X.11.d.16.12 and thence to road at X.11.d.55.16 and will rush RATION HOUSE and mop it up. Having done so they will leave 1 Section here as garrison and the

- 2 -

4. **METHOD OF ATTACK** Contd.

(a) "A" Company.

other Sections will proceed to get touch with Company on the left and with the MURAL FARM party.
No.2. Platoon will work from X.17.b.20.50 direct to MURAL FARM and rush the position from about X.17.b.40.60 and consolidate. A Lewis Gun post will be pushed well forward to cover remainder of platoon establishing posts from MURAL FARM to corner of hedge at X.11.d.90.00. and so joining up with Company on left.
No.3 Platoon will follow the two attacking Platoons from their assembly point and will proceed to X.17.b.20.50. They will establish a post here and thence proceed to clear hedges to the right and gain touch with the Division on our right.
No 4 Platoon will move forward at ZERO plus 3. to assembly position of Nos.1 and 2 Platoons and will thence move forward to about X.17.a.70.70. where they will be prepared to help either of the forward parties if they get hung up.
O.C., "A" Company will ensure that area marked Blue on map issued to him is clear of troops till ZERO plus 1 minute.

(b) Nos.9 and 10 Platoons with Nos. 7 and 8 Platoons will move at ZERO plus 15 and proceed along MURAL FARM road to about X.17.a.80.80. where they will half left turn and proceed to their objectives as laid down, following the enfilade barrage and clearing up any opposition.
No.11 Platoon will move from our old front line about X.11.b.80.07 and move in artillery formation to position about X.12.c.15.50.
No.8 Platoon will follow enfilade barrage and continue line of "C" Company on left on N.E. side of HEATON CROSS ROADS -BAILLEUL Road about X.12.c.20.10. and will get in touch with No.6.Platoon about S.7.d.20.60.
No.7. Platoon will follow No.6. and take up positions about X.12.c.20.50.

(c) At Zero plus 10, No.5 Platoon will proceed from assembly positions and will form up behind wall of SAUER KRAUTs FARM.
No.6 Platoon will form up in Sunken Road about S.7.b.10.20.
At Zero plus 20 No.6 Platoon will move forward and rush WIRRAL FARM from about S.7.d.65.80. while No.7. Platoon will be ready to assist and will establish touch with 1st Bn.R.Ir.Rifles about S.8.a.15.65.

(d) In each Platoon there will be told off 1 Section who will be responsible for mopping up the positions captured at once. They will also send back prisoners captured under small escort through Company Hqrs.to Battalion Hqrs.

5. As soon as MURAL FARM is taken a signal of two white very lights fired in quick succession towards our lines will be sent up. O.C., "D" Company will detail a reliable N.C.O. to establish a relay post about X.12.a.50.30. to pass this signal on to our left.
In the event of MURAL FARM not being taken the troops detailed to take RED LINE E.of MURAL to S.7.d.10.22. will not move, but WIRRAL will be taken in any case.
If WIRRAL is occupied and MURAL is not, O.C.,"B" Company will establish posts to connect WIRRAL with our trenches about X.12.a.

6. **PIONEERS.**
2 Companies 16th Bn.The R.Ir. Rifles(P) will put out wire in front of RED LINE when taken.
They are allotted as follows :-

"A" Company.	2 Platoons	on right.
"C"& ½ "B" Coys.	2 "	in centre.
½ "B" Company.	2 "	on left.

- 3 :-

6. **PIONEERS.** Contd.

They will be in our old front line trench behind their respective areas. On reaching and clearing objective, O.C., attacking Companies will at once send 2 guides per platoon to guide the party of Pioneers to their tasks.
The latter will provide their own covering parties.

7. **EQUIPMENT.**
The following will be carried :-
Two extra bandoliers per man.
2 Mills Bombs (No.5) per man for mopping up.
12 S.O.S. rockets per forward Platoon.
12 S.O.S. per Company Hqrs.
Wire cutters (all available)
Bill hooks.
Waterbottles filled.
3 Shovels and 1 pick per 5 men.

8. **CONTACT AEROPLANE.** Contact 'plane will fly over our positions at 4-45 a.m. on 22nd and at intervals later and will call for signals on KLAXON HORN. All ranks will indicate forward positions by all means. Platoon etc. Officers can do so by carefully spreading their maps in shell holes etc.

9. Before Zero, O.C., 107th Light Mortar Battery will have two guns in position about S.7.b.25.25. to fire on S.E. edge of WIRRAL if necessary.

10. Watches with synchronised time will be sent O.C., Companies before 10-0 p.m. on night of 21st.

11. 12(S)Bn.The Royal Irish Rifles are providing escort for prisoners from KOPJE FARM. Prisoners will be sent to there under small escort from Coys. Nothing except arms will be taken from the prisoners before they reach Battn. Hqrs.

12. **ADVANCE COMMAND POSTS.**
Advanced command posts will be established at X.11.c.90.52. for right and at X.5.a.97.15. for left. O.C., Companies will send messages there where they will be sent by wire or runner to KOPJE FARM. A Power Buzzer will be established at X.11.c.90.52. Wire will be laid from Battn. Hqrs. to this post but it will not be occupied till Zero plus 1.

13. **DRESSING STATION.** R.A.P. KOPJE FARM.

12 Noon
21/8/18.

Major,
Commanding 15th(S)Bn. The Royal Irish Rifles.

Summary of operations carried out by 15th (S)Bn. The Royal Irish Rifles on 21/22nd and 23rd Aug. 1918.

---

12 midnight. Received information all Companies in position and ready to move.

12-30 a.m. Gas projectors let off on MURAL FARM.

12-31 a.m. Artillery Barrage opened.

12-45 a.m. Received message timed 12-45 a.m. 'A B' i.e. Very Light sent up.
Received message from Forward Command post that no light had been sent up and that Lt. STEPHENSON'S Platoon had been unable to get round.

2-00 a.m. All objectives taken by "A" Company and touch was obtained with 8th Black Watch on right about X.17.a.35.30. and with "C" Company on left a few minutes later. No.2 Platoon had met with pretty severe opposition at beginning especially from machine guns from direction of POE CROSS. Our barrage ultimately dealt with this. No.1 Platoon met with opposition at RATION FARM and MURAL FARM but this was dealt with and some prisoners taken. Lt. STEPHENSON was wounded and as a result the signal could not be sent up from MURAL FARM.

2-10 a.m. "C" Company reached objectives and in touch with "A" and "D" Coys. on flanks.
Report confirming situation on right received from Liason Officer from 8th Black Watch stating that objectives on right had been reached and touch had been obtained with 9th Division.

2-30 a.m. Left Company reported WIRRAL FARM captured with very slight casualties.

3-30 a.m. "C" Company report objective gained and touch obtained on flanks.
16th Bn. The Royal Irish Rifles(P) reported having wired on front.

4-45 a.m. Reported to Brigade all objectives gained, touch established along line and wire out.

5.45 ~~4-50~~ a.m. Enemy counter-attacked on left Coy. front near WIRRAL FARM. Casualties were inflicted on enemy but he pushed in two of our posts. 2/Lieut. McDOWELL immediately organised a counter-attack and led it and drove the enemy out and re-established the line. A machine gun and some prisoners were captured in the counter-attack. During the counter-attack an enemy 'plane flew over our positions at a low height and fired on our line. Lewis Gun fire drove it off.

6-0 a.m. Our contact 'plane flew over our line and our dispositions were shewn to him.

During the day ~~strong~~ Stray shelling of our positions took place. A considerable number of "pineapples" were thrown at our left posts and along line where we joined up with the 1st Bn. The Royal Irish Rifles.

5-45 p.m. Enemy counter-attacked about S.18.a.90.70. but were driven off by Lewis Gun and rifle fire.

- 2 -

11-0 p.m.   Enemy put down barrage on our front line but it was mostly
            over our line. A heavier barrage was put down on our old
            front line, there was also a considerable amount of
            Machine Gun fire. Barrage on front line mostly 77 mm.&
            pineapples. On our old front line 4.2 and some 5.9's.
            Enemy attacked along our front from about X.17.b.20 -
            S.8.a.05.10.
            S.O.S. was sent up on left but our artillery did not
            open properly for 13 minutes. Enemy attacked in groups
            and were driven off by Lewis Gun and rifle fire. One
            wounded prisoner taken belonged to 63rd Regt.
            Counter attack took place during relief and in the
            centre of our line some of the posts were doubled and had
      four two Lewis Guns. With the very bright night the shooting
            must have been quite good and all posts report many
            casualties inflicted.

12 midnight.
23rd.   Everything quiet.

1.45 pm   Relief reported complete and Battn. withdrew to Reserve.

3.45 pm   Battn. reported in Reserve positions.

            Our Casualties were very slight, as far as ascertained
            up to the present.
            Officers.   3 Wounded.
            O.R.   4 Killed
                           40 Wounded.
            I have not yet got result of check from Companies.

                    General.

            Our relay post at about X.12.a.30.25. reported two white
            lights sent up from MURAL, shortly after barrage started.
            They thought these were our signals and passed them on.
            Forward command post report that owing to smoke and dust
            no lights were visable or could be seen. This would show
            that some other type of signal should be devised for such
            operations.

                                            [signature]

23/8/18.   Major,
                                  Commanding 15th(S)Bn. The Royal Irish Rifles.

Enemy barrage during operations on
21/22 Aug. 1918.

ZERO plus 8.   Barrage of T.M. put down along our front line from about X.II.b.90.10, to left.

" " 10.   4.2 barrage along front line and on support.

" " 12.   5.9 joined this barrage.

" " 25.   77 mm. barrage started on No Mans Land about 60^k in front of our line.

Barrage was pretty thin and was very slow in being put down.

23/8/18.

[signature]

Major,
Commanding 15 th(S)Bn. The Royal Irish Rifles.

WAR DIARY
INTELLIGENCE SUMMARY
(Erase heading not required.)

15 R. Irish Rifles
Vol 36

Army Form C. 2118.

Place	Date	Hour	Summary of Events and Information	Remarks and references to Appendices
MONT NOIR	Sept 1st		The following awards received for gallantry and devotion to duty in the action on 21/22nd August were announced:— Bar to M.M. 15/16546 C.S.M. S. HARRISON M.M. "C" Coy. 17/1860 Rfm R.B. PATTERSON. M.M. "A" Coy. Military Medal 15/12128 Sgt F. ROSS "B" Coy. 15/593 Cpl J. BELL "A" Coy. 43039 L/Cpl A. BRAND "A" Coy. 14/16274 Rfm E. BRUCE "B" Coy. 16/8 Rfm R. DOBBIN. 14/6715 Rfm A. MURRAY "A" Coy. 17/790 Rfm W. LOWRY "A" Coy. 52394 Rfm J. JONES "B" Coy. 14/542b Rfm J. McKEE "A" Coy. 52312 Rfm J. GREANEY "B" Coy. Fine but much cooler. Kit inspections and settling into billets. Orders arrived at 3 p.m. that the Battn was to move at 8 p.m. The 109th Brigade was to relieve the 108th Brigade in Divisional Support the 108th relieving the 109th Bde in the line. Battn arrived at MAGILLIGAN CAMP at 10.30 p.m.	
	2nd		Some heavy showers. Everyone engaged making quarters more comfortable. One Platoon per Coy was occupied repairing the tracks near their billets. Revd HALLIHAN. M.C. C.F. joined the Battn.	
	3rd		Weather fine. Demonstration of artillery formation by "A" Coy. Battn moved to new billets at 7 p.m. BHQ. S.18 d.05.00. "A" Coy. T.13.c.70.70. B Coy T.13 a.70.00. "C" Coy S.18 a.70.70 D Coy S.18 2.10.20.	

J.J. McEntarise
Lieut.-Colonel
Commanding 15th (S) Battn. The Royal Irish Rifles

WAR DIARY
INTELLIGENCE SUMMARY.

(Erase heading not required.)

Army Form C. 2118.

Instructions regarding War Diaries and Intelligence Summaries are contained in F. S. Regs., Part II. and the Staff Manual respectively. Title pages will be prepared in manuscript.

Place	Date	Hour	Summary of Events and Information	Remarks and references to Appendices
51B 10500	Sept 4th		Weather dull and showery. Everybody engaged making quarters more comfortable.	
	5th		Glorious day.	
	6th		The following casualties received. Lt Col R.E. SMYTHE D.S.O., Wounded (Gas) Revd HALLIHAN M.C., C.F. Wounded (Gas) Lieut A.N. ANDERSON the A/Adjt. Wounded (Gas) 2nd Lieut S.D. IRONS. Wounded (Gas) 2nd Lieut J. McCAUSLAND Wounded (Gas)	
	7th		Lieut W.G. WOOD R.A.M.C. Wounded (Gas). Major E.R.H. MAY assumed command. Lieut W.H. WYLES and 2nd Lieut E.C. THOMPSON Wounded (Gas). 2nd Lt Wounded (Gas)	
BAILLEUL PLOEGSTEERT I/10000.	8th	7.12 pm T.U.C.	Battn. moved into Bde Support. A & C Coys relieved Coys of the 12th Norfolk Regt. D & B Coys relieved 1st R.I.R. R.I.F. H.Q. T. 10. 6-8080.	
	9th		Weather very wet. Wounded (Gas) 1 O.R.	
	10th		Weather still bad. Wounded 2 O.R.	
	11th		Dry but cloudy. Wounded (Gas) 10 O.R.	
PLOEGSTEERT BELGIUM 4/40000	12th		The Battn relieved the 1st R.I.R. R.I.F. in Hill 63 Sector. Wounded 5 O.R.	
	13th		Quiet day.	
	14th		Wounded 6 O.R.	
28 SN4 27 SE 28 SW	15th		Relieved by the 9th R. INNIS. FUS. Casualties. The Major & 2nd Lieut S. GATENSBY & 1 O.R. Wounded 2 O.R. Killed	

P.J. McSherran
Lieut.-Colonel,
Commanding 15th (S) Battn, The Royal Irish Rifles

Army Form C. 2118.

WAR DIARY
INTELLIGENCE SUMMARY.
(Erase heading not required.)

Instructions regarding War Diaries and Intelligence Summaries are contained in F. S. Regs., Part II. and the Staff Manual respectively. Title pages will be prepared in manuscript.

Place	Date	Hour	Summary of Events and Information	Remarks and references to Appendices
Sheet 27 R27 & 60 B.O.	Sept 16th		Battn. in billets at MESSHOVEK near the old front line. Day devoted to cleaning and inspections.	
	17th		Weather fine. Companies training under Coy arrangements. 2nd Lieut J KNOX M.C. awarded Bar to M.C. for conspicuous gallantry on 21/22nd August. 2nd Lieut W.J. McDOWELL awarded MC.	
	18th		Weather fine. Companies training.	
TERDEGHEM	19th		Battalion moved to new billets near TERDEGHEM.	
ESQUELBECQ	20th		Battalion moved to billets in ESQUELBECQ area.	
	21st		Resting and cleaning up.	
	22nd		Training under Coy arrangements. Orders received to be prepared to move at a moments notice.	
	23rd		Weather fine. Training in the morning under Coy arrangements. Advance party left to reconnoitre new billeting area.	
	24th		Lt.Col.B.J. JONES. D.S.O. from 6th LEINSTERS joined and assumed command. Major J.M. McCALLUM D.S.O. returned from leave.	
	25th		Lt. M.O.C. Mr presented ribbons to NCOs & the awarded decorations. Major E.R.HAY D.S.O. M.C. [illegible] 2i/c in Command, 1st R.Ir.Rif.	

R.A McClesney
Lieut.-Colonel,
Commanding 15th (S) Battn, The Royal Irish Rifles

Army Form C. 2118.

WAR DIARY

~~INTELLIGENCE~~ SUMMARY

(Erase heading not required.)

Place	Date	Hour	Summary of Events and Information	Remarks and references to Appendices
27/F 2, 7 a.1, 9.	Sept 26th		Battalion moved to TUNNELLERS CAMP in the PROVEN area. The batt'n was shelled coming through PROVEN. Casualties: 1 Killed, 3 OR Wounded & missing	
28/A 22 & 91	27th		Battalion moved to BRONNE CAMP. Orders received to be prepared to move in Battle Order from 10 A.m. 28th inst.	
28/B/c 20.20	28th		Battalion moved to trenches and dugouts at HELLFIRE CORNER	
	29th		Battalion less transport moved to WESTHOEK J7.d.70.00. Transport & H. Stores stopped at HELLFIRE CORNER	
	30th		Battalion moved to BECELAERE.	

                                        [signature]
                                        Lieut.-Colonel,
                                        Commanding 15th (S) Batt'n., The Royal Irish Rifles

WAR DIARY or INTELLIGENCE SUMMARY

Army Form C. 2118.

15th R.I.R. O.R.

Vol 37

Place	Date	Hour	Summary of Events and Information	Remarks and references to Appendices
	1918			
TERHAND	Oct 1st		Battalion relieved 1st ROYAL IRISH RIFLES in Brigade Support at dusk took Battalion H.Q. at K.21.d.9.8. Casualties – 11 ORs Wounded. 2 ORs Killed. REV. P. WATSON C.F. Wounded at duty.	C.A.R/L.St.
	2nd		Battalion moved in close support to 1st Roy IRISH RIFLES 107th Battalion Headquarters at CAVENDISH HOUSE K.29.a.80.80. Battalion at dusk to positions of previous day. Casualties 4 ORs Killed. 32 ORs Wounded.	C.A.R.
	3rd		In Brigade Support at Same place. Quiet day. Great aerial activity. Casualties – 10 ORs.	C.A.R.
	4th		Battalion relieved 1st R. IRISH RIFLES in front line. Battalion Hd. at K.29.b.20.80. Brigade Complete. 28.30 Casualties Wounded. "C" + "D" Companies in front line. "A" Coy in support – 10th Brigade on Left. 29th Brigade on Right.	C.A.R.
	5th		Battalion attacked to limits of 104th and 105th Infantry Brigades Battalion from line. Battalion moved into area (Sheet 29) J.10 b 11. J.16.a. + b. J.11.a. + b. Battalion Hd. at J.12.d.95.80. Casualties 2 ORs Killed. 6 ORs Wounded.	C.A.R.
	6th		Battalion in Same area. Reorganisation. Supplying carried out. trenches good. Casualties 2 ORs Wounded.	C.A.R.
	7th		In Same area. Quiet day. Casualties – Nil.	C.A.R.
	8th		Battalion moves to POLYGON BUTTS area with Battalion Hd. at J.10.a.50.60. Aeroplane arches forced landing at Cross Roads at J.12.d.10.50. Reserve orders kept in case of attack. Battalion will move up to and defend TERHAND RIDGE. Casualties. Nil.	C.A.R.
POLYGON BUTTS	9th		Orders in case of attack cancelled. Battalion form part of Mobile Reserve at crossroads of Brigadier General Commandant. Training carried out. Casualties. Nil.	

Lieut.-Colonel,
Commanding 15th (S) Battn., The Royal Irish Rifles.

Army Form C. 2118.

WAR DIARY
or
INTELLIGENCE SUMMARY.
(Erase heading not required.)

Instructions regarding War Diaries and Intelligence
Summaries are contained in F. S. Regs., Part II.
and the Staff Manual respectively. Title pages
will be prepared in manuscript.

Place	Date	Hour	Summary of Events and Information	Remarks and references to Appendices
POLYGON BUTTS	1918 Oct. 10th		In same area. Training. Casualties Nil.	C.4.R.
	11th		In same area. Training. Casualties Nil.	C.4.R.
	12th		In same area Training. Officers reinforcements 108th Brigade arrived. Capt. C.N.L. STRONGE. M.C. assumed	C.4.R.
			the duties of Adjutant vice Capt. C.M. CASTLE. M.C. to Brigade Employ. Casualties Nil.	C.4.R.
	13th		Battalion leaves Area at 18.30 and goes by march route to overnight assembly positions. Battalion	
			H.W. DIME HOUSE T.24.a.80.60. Companies from up C- Right Front D. Left Front.	
			B- Support. A- Reserve. Casualties - 8 OR's wounded.	C.9.R
	14th		Attack starts at 05.35. Everything goes well and objective reached in good time. Companies	
			Consolidate E of MOORSEELE. Battalion HQ established at 08.00 at SILVER FARM L.22.b.30.25	
			were pushed at 10.30 to horse at L.23.b.30.60 in MOORSEELE. 1st ROY IRISH RIFLES saw	
			through Battalion at 09.00 and 2nd ROY IRISH RIFLES pass through in Support. 1st Battalion	
			received outskirts of GULLEGHEM entered for little where heavily during night. Casualties	
			4 ORs Killed 42 ORs wounded 3 ORs Missing 2 Officers wounded Lieut. J.M. NAPIER Lieut W.J. MORRISON.	
	15th		Battalion move into Brigade Reserve and taken on duties of Honor & Guards in positions SE of GULLEGHEM	C.9.R
			take no in line and Consolidate from G.21.L.04 to C.34. 2nd in Brigade with DURHAM LIGHT INFANTRY	
			on right and 1st ROY IRISH RIFLES on left. Battalion HQ in GULLEGHEM. Pte. Bell late Bn. M.G.	
			Casualties 2 ORs Killed. 1 Officer (Rev. R. WATSON CF) MW ORs	
			Wounded. 1 OR Missing	

W.G. Rodwell
Lieut.-Colonel
Commanding 15th (S) Battn., The Royal Irish Rifles.

Army Form C. 2118.

WAR DIARY
or
INTELLIGENCE SUMMARY.
(Erase heading not required.)

Place	Date	Hour	Summary of Events and Information	Remarks and references to Appendices
	1918 Oct. 16th		Battalion moved to ROLLEGHEM CAPPEL F.28.c. Battalion HQ at F.28.c.10.50. QM Stores and Transport refrom battalion. "A" Company moved to relieve of TWIG FARM K.24.c. to act as Burial and Salvage party. Casualties 1 OR Accidly Killed. 2 ORs wounded.	C.q.R
	17th		At ROLLEGHEM CAPPEL. Reorganised and re-equipped. Casualties NIL.	C.q.R
	18		Battalion moved to LINDELEDE area. HQ at B.14.f.70.90. "C" Company billeted out of WEbb at B.20.9.9.0. Casualties :- Wounded (Gas) 22 ORs	C.q.R
	19th		Battalion addressed by Divisional Commander. Move to area B.19.a+b (Sheet 29). Casualties NIL.	C.q.R
	20th		Move at 01.30 to assembly positions at Road in C.26.b.1.d. Battalion HQ at C.20.c.60.30. Formed up for attack as follows:- "B" Company - Centre Front. "D" Company - Left Front. "A" Company Right Front. "C" Company in Support with "C" Company 1st ROYAL IRISH RIFLES in Reserve. Attack starts at 06.00. Battalion reaches approximate objective namely GAVERBEKE at 09.00. Lieut-Col D.JONES D.S.O. Capt. H.G. MORROW MC 2nd Lieut. W. ANDERSON Killed. 2nd Lieut. J. KNOX MC. Died of Wounds. Capt. C.N.L. STRONGE MC Adjutant - Wounded. Capt. F.M. GAUNT. of "A" Company assumes temporary Command 1st ROY. IR RIFLES from Rough Battalion at 17.00 to continue attack. Battalion bivouacs to Brigade Reserve in area (Sheet 29) I.2. Bn. Battalion HQ at I.2.c.80.15. Major J.D.M.MCCALLUM D.S.O.	C.q.R

V.D. Bate
Lieut.-Colonel,
Commanding 15th (S) Battn. The Royal Irish Rifles

WAR DIARY
or
INTELLIGENCE SUMMARY

Army Form C. 2118.

Place	Date	Hour	Summary of Events and Information	Remarks and references to Appendices
	20th (contd)		assumed command, vice Capt. F.M.GAUNT. Casualties 3 Offs. 12 O.Rs killed. 1 Off. 50 O.Rs wounded. 7 O.Rs Missing.	C.q.R.
	21st		In same area. Lieut-Colonel B.T.JONES D.S.O. & Major H.G. MORROW M.C. buried at I.2.c.00.05. Companies reorganised. "C" Company attached to 1st ROY. IR. RIFLES. Casualties - Nil.	C.q.R.
	22nd		Battalion moves into Brigade support at 08.00 to support and form left flank guard for 2nd Division. "B" Company in front. ROYAL IR. RIFLES with Battalion HQ. at I.11.c.10.10. Dispositions:- "B" Company in front D & A Companies - the latter with left on E. bank of GAVERBEKE at I.11.d. Central with "B" Company's right at I.13.d.Central in touch with 2nd. ROY. IRISH RIFLES. Lieut F.D.WILLIAMS M.C. found and took over duties of Adjutant. Capt. W.SOMERS M.C. buried & took Command of "A" Coy. Casualties:- 2.O.Rs killed. 4 Offs (Capt. F.M. GAUNT. 2nd Lieut B.STOW. Lieut G.A.McFARLAND & 2nd Lieut C.B.McCOMB) + 57 O.Rs wounded. 2.O.Rs missing. 2/Lt. B.STOW. died of wounds.	
	23rd		Enemy reported retiring at 03.00. Civilians coming into our line report Enemy retiring E. of HEINWEG - WAEREGHEM railway. Orders to concentrate Battalion at Ross' junction N.E. of KNOCK. Concentration completed and Battalion came into support to 1st. IR. RIFLES who were breaching as Advance Guard and supported by French Cavalry. Orders received by wily of 107th Brigade to 109th Brigade. Battalion orders to move to area W. of	C.q.R.

Y.W.O. Russell
Lieut.-Colonel.
Commanding 15th (S) Battn. The Royal Irish Rifles.

WAR DIARY
or
INTELLIGENCE SUMMARY.
(Erase heading not required.)

Army Form C. 2118.

Instructions regarding War Diaries and Intelligence Summaries are contained in F. S. Regs. Part II. and the Staff Manual respectively. Title pages will be prepared in manuscript.

Place	Date	Hour	Summary of Events and Information	Remarks and references to Appendices
	23 (cont)		R LYS and Ed HULSTE without incident. Battalion on relief. Companies moved off and then billeted in village of OYGHEM. Casualties. 1 OR wounded. 1 Off (2nd Lt J Knox) died of wounds.	
	24th		Quiet day. Companies fitted out. Spent time in cleaning up and refitting. Lieut-Colonel W.Mc.C.CROSBIE. D.S.O (Royal Munster Fusiliers) joined and took over Command of Battalion. Casualties NIL	C-a-R
	25th		Under Company arrangements. Billets inspected by Brigadier General Commanding. Battalion paraded at 12.00. Commanding Officers read out Congratulatory orders by Marshal FOCH and Lieut-General JACOBS (Corps Commander) on truth of all that in Division in recent offensive. At 16.45 orders received to move forward into close support to 108th Brigade. Battalion moved at 18.00 and went into billets in farms in neighbourhood of EVANGELIEBOOM S of WAEREGHEM - HARLEBEKE railway. Move completed at 21.20. Transport and Rear HQ which had moved in morning to OYGHEM moved forward to Farms E.N.W. of WAEREGHEM - HARLEBEKE railway. Casualties - NIL. Congratulatory message received from Army Commander.	C-a-R
	26th		Battalion moved at 14.30 to LENDELEDE area. Companies occupied same billets as on 18th instant. Weather fine. Casualties. NIL.	C-a-R
	27th		Battalion moved to BELLEGHEM by march route, passing starting point at 10.00. Battalion HQ at (Sheet 29) N.27.c.3.8. Companies in Area N.26 + 27. Move completed by 17.00. Casualties NIL.	C-a-R
	28th		Same area. Cleaning up &c. Weather very fine. Casualties. NIL	C-a-R
	29th		Same area. Parties. Platoon Training under Brigade PT Instructor. Casualties. NIL	C-a-R
	30th		Same area. PJ under Brigade PP Instructor. Weather fine. Casualties. NIL	C-a-R
	31st		Same area. Training under Company arrangements. Weather wet and cold.	C-a-R

Wm G Roskie
Lieut-Colonel,
Commanding 15th (S) Battn., The Royal Irish Rifles

WAR DIARY
OF
INTELLIGENCE SUMMARY.

(Erase heading not required.)

Army Form C. 2118.

15 R. Irish Rifles
Vol 38

Place	Date 1918 Nov.	Hour	Summary of Events and Information	Remarks and references to Appendices
BELLEGHEM	1st		Battalion moves from BELLEGHEM area to RECKEM with Battalion H.Q. at 7.29 a 90.50. Battalion moves by march route passing starting point at 16.00 hours arriving at new billets at 19.00 hours. Weather fine. Casualties = Nil.	cuts
RECKEM	2nd		Same area. Companies under Company arrangements. Weather - rainy. Casualties - Nil.	cuts
	3rd		Battalion moves by march route to MOUSCRON area. - RISQUONS TOUT - Battalion H.Q. M.14.a.20.90. Battalion passed starting point 09.00 and arrived at new billets 10.00. Very good billets. Weather - occasional showers. Casualties - Nil.	cuts
MOUSCRONS TOUT	4th		Same area. Companies under Company arrangements. Weather fine. Casualties - Nil. Capt. R.F. CLARKE CF. joined Battalion.	cuts
	5th		Battalion bathed at MOUSCRON. Weather - wet. Casualties - Nil. Lieut. F. FARRELL joined Battalion.	cuts
	6th		Same area. Companies under Company arrangements. Weather dull. Casualties "Nil". Capt. L.S. DUNCAN. M.C. returned from leave. Capt. F.G. UPRICHARD joined Battalion.	cuts
	7th		Same area. Companies under Company arrangements. Weather dull and wet. Casualties - Nil.	cuts
	8th		Same area. Companies under Company arrangements. Weather dull. Casualties - Nil.	cuts
	9th		Same area. Company arrangements. Brigade Sports. Weather fine. Casualties Nil.	cuts
	10th		Same area. Church Parade. Brigade rifle Cinema - Nil.	cuts
	11th		Same area. Battalion parade 11am. Official news "HOSTILITIES CEASE" 11.00 "this day". Battalion football match v. 9th Royal Irish Fusiliers - 15th Rifles won 4-0. Casualties Nil. Weather wet.	cuts
	12th		Same area. Brigade parade 11am. - rehearsal for Inspection by Divisional Commander. Weather - fine. Lieut. P.A. McELWAINE proceeded on leave. Lt. HOMFREE returned from leave. Casualties - Nil.	cuts
	13th		Same area. Brigade Inspected by Divisional Commander. Divisional Commander presents medal ribbons. Weather fine. Casualties Nil.	cuts

W. G. Trodie
Lieut.-Colonel,
Commanding 15th (S) Batt., The Royal Irish Rifles

WAR DIARY or INTELLIGENCE SUMMARY

Army Form C. 2118.

Place	Date 1918 Nov.	Hour	Summary of Events and Information	Remarks and references to Appendices
	14th	13.30	Same area. Brigade route march about 7 miles. left starting point 10.30. returned 5 kills. Weather fine. Casualties - NIL. Football Match 15th R.I.R. v. 108th Field Amb. result 15th R.I.R. 3 108th F.A. 0.	WJS
	15th		Same area. Companies under Company arrangements. Weather fine. Casualties - NIL.	
	16th		Same area. Attended by Rev. C.F. CLARKE C.F. on Educational Scheme. Weather fine. Casualties - NIL.	
	17th		Same area. Church Parade. Special Thanks Giving Service held at ROUBAIX. Weather fine but cold. Casualties - NIL.	
	18th		Same area. Companies under Company arrangements. Lt. R. BAILLIE joined. Weather wet and cold. Casualties - NIL.	
	19th		Same area. Companies under Company arrangements. Capt. C.N.L. STRONGE M.C. returned from Sick leave. Weather wet and cold. Casualties - NIL.	
	20th		Same area. Brigade route march. Weather very misty and damp all day. Casualties - NIL.	
	21st		Same area. Companies under Company arrangements. Weather misty and damp. Casualties - NIL.	WJS
	22nd		Same area. Brigade day. Advance Guard Scheme. Football Match 9th Royal Inniskilling Fusiliers v. 15th Royal Irish Rifles. Resu't. 9th R. IN. Fus. 2 : 15th R.I.R. 1. Weather fine. Casualties - NIL. Lt. H.J. WALSHE joined Battalion.	
	23rd		Captain's Parade and Kit Inspection. Weather fine. Casualties - NIL.	
	24th	3.15	Same area. Church Parade. Weather fine. Rugby Match 15th Rifles v. 36th Bn R.A. Result 15th R.I.R. (Lieut. WALLACE = 1 goal) - 36th Bn. R.A. - 0 pts. Casualties - NIL. Weather fine.	WJS
	25th		Same area. Battalion School holds first class. "A" + "B" Companies attend School - "C" + "D" Companies on ranges. Weather drill and cold. Casualties - NIL.	
	26th		Same area. Brigade Advance Guard Scheme. Order of March 15th R.Ir.Rif. "D" Company doing duty as Vanguard. 1st Roy. Ir. Rifles. 2nd. Roy. Ir. Rifles. Weather misty but dull. Casualties - NIL. Billets inspected by Lieut. W.L. COOPER. + F.W. MARSHALL. M.C. and 2nd. Lt. A.O. WARD joined Battalion.	WJS
	27th		Same area. Companies under Company arrangements. Football Soccer 15th Rifles. 5 goals 110th Field Ambulance 1. Weather drill cold. Casualties - NIL.	
	28th		Same area. Companies under Company arrangements. Weather drill and cold. Casualties - NIL. Football = HQ 3. v. No 10 O.C.S. 2.	
	29th		Same area. Commanding Officers Parade. Battalion drill. Weather drill and cold. Casualties - NIL.	
	30th		Same area. Brigade Advance Guard Scheme. Order of march 2nd R.Ir. Rifles. Brigade H.Q. 1st R.Ir. Rifles. 15th R.Ir Rifles. 107th L.M.B. Regimental Transport Brigade. Weather fine. Casualties - NIL.	

Bn. G. Rodi
Lieut.-Colonel,
Commanding 15th (S) Battn., The Royal Irish Rifles.

15 Irish Rifles

Army Form C. 2118.

C. A. Kinsford Lt. I.O.

96 B 39

WAR DIARY
or
INTELLIGENCE SUMMARY.
(Erase heading not required.)

Instructions regarding War Diaries and Intelligence Summaries are contained in F. S. Regs., Part II. and the Staff Manual respectively. Title pages will be prepared in manuscript.

Place	Date 1918	Hour	Summary of Events and Information	Remarks and references to Appendices
PISQUON TOUT.	Dec 1		Church Parades. Weather cold & fine. Soccer 15th R.I.R. v civilians of Tourcoing. 15th R.I.R. 10 goals TOURCOING 0	
	2		Company parades, education reports. Rugby Match. 2nd R.I.R. v 15th R.I.R. Result: 15th R.I.R 24 pts. 2nd R.I.R 26. Weather dull	
	3		Brigade Parade. Weather fine. Soccer. 15th R.I.R. v 144th F. Amb Result: 15th R.I.R 4 goals. 144th F.A. 1 goal. Battn. Route March. Weather wet.	
	4		Company parades. Rugby Match 1st R.I.R. v 15th R.I.R. 1st R.I.R. 6 pts. 15th I.R. 3 pts. Soccer Match 109th F. Amb. v 15th R.I.R. Result: 15th R.I.R. 5 goals. 109th F. Amb 0. Weather dull.	
	5		Divisional parade. Division march past. Divl commander in column of companies. Weather fine.	
	6		Company arrangements. 13.5 when proceeded to ROUBAIX to line the streets whilst His Majesty the King of England drove through. Weather fine.	
	7		Battn moves to MOUSCRON with B.H.Q in Rue de Tourcoing. Billeting good.	
	8		Weather fine	

J. Munro Call
Major.
Commanding 15th (S) Battn, The Royal Irish Rifles

Army Form C. 2118.

WAR DIARY
or
INTELLIGENCE SUMMARY.
(Erase heading not required.)

Instructions regarding War Diaries and Intelligence Summaries are contained in F.S. Regs., Part II. and the Staff Manual respectively. Title pages will be prepared in manuscript.

Place	Date 1916	Hour	Summary of Events and Information	Remarks and references to Appendices
MOUSCRON	Dec 9		Companies under Company Commanders. Trench Grove de Guire à l'Orme Corps. Major J.D. McCallum D.S.O. a l'Orme. Brigade HQ N° 32. Bjn. A.E. Williamson, a l'Orme Regt. Lt. Fy. Day 78/32x0. Bjn. D. McAtamney. Weather fine.	
	10.		Companies under company arrangements. Played first round Duel Sweep-bup against 1st Rifles. Result 1-1. Weather dull.	
	11.		Companies under company arrangements. Weather fine. Batn. Route March. Weather fine.	
	12.			
	13.		Replayed tie against 1st R.I.R. Result: 15th R.I.R. 1. 1st R.I.R.O. Weather wet.	
	14.		Companies under Company Commanders. Kit Inspections etc. Weather dull.	
	15.		Church Parades. Weather fine.	
	16.		Inspection of Division by Corps Commander Lt Gen Benoir de Lisle XVth Corps. The Division was complimented on the "Turnout & March Past". Weather showery.	
	17.		Companies under Company arrangements. Weather fine.	

L.A. Kingston Lt I.O.

journal a tr

Major

Commanding 15th (S) Battn., The Royal Irish Rifles.

Army Form C. 2118.

WAR DIARY
or
INTELLIGENCE SUMMARY.
(Erase heading not required.)

C.A. Kinsford Lt & I.O.

Place	Date 1917	Hour	Summary of Events and Information	Remarks and references to Appendices
MOUSCRON	Dec. 18.		Companies under Company arrangements. Played 2nd R.I.R. in Sole Final of Divl Soccer Competition. Result:- 15th R.I.R. 2 goals. 2nd R.I.R. 0.	
	19.		Companies under Company arrangements. Weather fine.	
	20.		Battn addressed by Divl Commander. Weather fine.	
	21.		Battn Ceremonial Parade at RISQUONS TOUT. Brigade Boxing Competition. Kit Inspection. Weather very cold.	
	22.		Church Parade. Weather dull.	
	23.		Companies under Company arrangements. Weather wet.	
	24.		Brig. General's Inspection. Company Photographs taken. Brig. General & Staff dined at Battn H.Q. Weather. Rain & Sleet.	
	25.		Christmas Day. Church Parade & Christmas Dinners. Bgde S.C. 107 Brigade went round Balln. Weather dull.	
	26.		1 O.R. 10710 Lt. M.B. died in 15th R.I.R. Guard Room. General Holiday. Weather. Early morning frost.	

J. Cwellff Major
Commanding 15th (S) Battn, The Royal Irish Rifles

Army Form C. 2118.

WAR DIARY
or
INTELLIGENCE SUMMARY.
(Erase heading not required.)

Instructions regarding War Diaries and Intelligence Summaries are contained in F. S. Regs., Part II. and the Staff Manual respectively. Title pages will be prepared in manuscript.

Place	Date 1918	Hour	Summary of Events and Information	Remarks and references to Appendices
MOUSCRON	Dec. 27		Day devoted to cleaning equipment.	
	28.		Weather wet.	
			Kit inspections & cleaning up.	
			Weather wet.	
	29.		Church Parade.	
			Weather wet.	
	30.		Company commanders arrangements & education.	
			Football. 15th R.I.R. v 109th Field Amb. Result: 15th R.I.R. 2 goals against 0.	
			Weather wet.	
	31.		Company commanders arrangements & Education	
			Weather wet.	

C.G. Knoxford Lt & I.O.

John Gallen Major
Commanding 15th (S) Battn., ...

No. 3/26.
ORDERLY ROOM
1 FEB 1919
15th

15 R Irish Regt
Army Form C. 2118.
Vol 40

WAR DIARY
or
INTELLIGENCE SUMMARY.
(Erase heading not required.)

Instructions regarding War Diaries and Intelligence Summaries are contained in F.S. Regs., Part II. and the Staff Manual respectively. Title pages will be prepared in manuscript.

Place	Date	Hour	Summary of Events and Information	Remarks and references to Appendices
MOUSCRON	1919 Jan 1.		General holiday. Weather wet	cuts
"	2.		Companies under Capt Wynham & Educational Classes. Rugby Match 109th Bde v 108th Bde. Score 109th Bde 3pts against 0. Weather showery	cuts
"	3.		Battn Route March. Weather showery	cuts
"	4.		Kit inspections & Education. Weather wet	cuts
"	5.		Church Parades. Weather wet	cuts
"	6.		Company training & Education. 2. 0.12 men demobilised	cuts
"	7.		Bde Rugby Match agst 109th Bde. Result Lost. 109 Bde 6pts 107 Bde 3pts. Weather fine	cuts
"	8.		Company training & Education. Weather fine	cuts
"	9.		Company training & Education. Weather fine	cuts
"	10.		Company training & Education. Weather fine	cuts
			16. Ex inspection of Coys 10.00 Brigade Route March starting point 11.20 - Miles 13.00 11.8.12 — medical	cuts

J French Capt
Commanding 15th (S) Battn. The Royal Irish Regt

Army Form C. 2118.

WAR DIARY
or
INTELLIGENCE SUMMARY.
(Erase heading not required.)

Instructions regarding War Diaries and Intelligence Summaries are contained in F. S. Regs. Part II. and the Staff Manual respectively. Title pages will be prepared in manuscript.

Place	Date	Hour	Summary of Events and Information	Remarks and references to Appendices
MOUSCRON	1919 Jan 10 (contd)		Lt. Col. R.C. Smythe D.S.O. late a/a 15th R.I.R. arrived C.W.S.	appx
	" 11		Weather fine	
			Kit inspection & Education	
			Weather fine	appx
			8 O.R. demobilised	
	" 12		Church Parade.	appx
			Belgian Croix de Guerre awarded to:-	
			Capt. J.J. Hill M.C.	
			Rev. R. Watson C.F.	
			12505 Cpl. J.A. Aitken	appx
			1514 Bgn. J. McKane	
			13146 Bgn. J. McCullough	
			11 O.R. were awarded.	
	" 13		Weather dull.	
			Coy. training & Education.	appx
			Weather dull.	
	" 14		Coy. training & Education.	appx
			Weather fine.	
	" 15		Coy. training & Education	
			Rugby Match - 36th (Ulster) Divn. v 36th Divn. (Australian) Artillery (Lt. J. Wallace R.A.M.C	appx
			& 10th S. Kenton) Result: Divn. 13pts - Australians 3pts.	
			Weather fine.	

F.J. Hill Lt Col
Commanding 15th (S) Battn. The Royal Irish Rifles

WAR DIARY or INTELLIGENCE SUMMARY

Army Form C. 2118.

Place	Date	Hour	Summary of Events and Information	Remarks and references to Appendices
MOUSCRON	1919 Jan. 16		Company training & Education. Brigade Cross Country Running Competition. Result 1st 15th 12, 2nd 12.1.12. Weather fine	AWS
	" 17		Company training & Education. Weather showery	AWS
	" 18		Kit inspection & Education. Divisional Cross Country Running Competition. Lt. Col. W. McCrostie D.S.O. proceeded on special leave. Major F.D. McCallum D.S.O. took over command of the Battn. Weather fine	AWS
	" 19		Church Parade. Lieut R. Bates left for demobilisation. Rugby match:- 36th (Ulster) Division v 2nd Life Guards. Winners M.J. Battn. Scrum J Wallace 2nd Q and Thornton played for the Division. Kicks: Drew 2, 3pts Life Guards 3 pts. Weather dull.	AWS
	" 20		1 O.R. demobilised today. Company training & Education. Lieut. W.L. Cooper left for demobilisation. Lt. W.L. Cosgrove demobilised today. Weather fine	AWS
	" 21		Coy. training & Education. 2/Lieut R.D. Watkins R.E. left for demobilisation 3 O.Rs demobilised. Weather fine	AWS

April Capt.

Commanding 13th (S) Battn. The Royal Irish Rifles

Army Form C. 2118.

WAR DIARY
or
INTELLIGENCE SUMMARY
(Erase heading not required.)

Instructions regarding War Diaries and Intelligence Summaries are contained in F. S. Regs. Part II. and the Staff Manual respectively. Title pages will be prepared in manuscript.

Place	Date 1919	Hour	Summary of Events and Information	Remarks and references to Appendices
MOUSCRON	Jan. 22		Company training & Education. Major J.D. McCallum D.S.O. proceeds to England on leave. Capt. J.F. Kiln M.C. takes over command of the Battalion. Weather March. 15 &12.1.R. v. 122 Coy. 12.E. Result 13th D.L.R. 5 goals v. R.I.goal.	cuts
	23		Weather dull. Recruits & Strong kept for demobilisation. F.O.16 demobilised this day. Coy training & Education. Weather dull.	cuts
	24		Coy training & Education. Meritorious Service Medal awarded to:- 9/13446 Cpl. M. Rutley 1/1 353 Sgt. A.E. Thompson 13131 Bgn. D. McWilliams	cuts
	25		Weather dull. Kit inspection & Education. 2 O.R's demobilised.	cuts
	26		Weather dull. Church Parades. Weather snowy. Boys under Coy arrangements.	cuts
	27		Weather cold. 3/Lt. A.O. Warr this day proceeds to England for demobilisation. 35 O.R's were demobilised this day.	cuts

Signature Capt.
Commanding 1st/4th Battn. The Royal Irish Rifles.

Army Form C. 2118.

WAR DIARY
or
INTELLIGENCE SUMMARY.
(Erase heading not required.)

Instructions regarding War Diaries and Intelligence Summaries are contained in F. S. Regs., Part II. and the Staff Manual respectively. Title pages will be prepared in manuscript.

Place	Date 1919	Hour	Summary of Events and Information	Remarks and references to Appendices
MOUSCRON	Jan 28		Coys under Company arrangements. Wash'd cots fuel & rat'ns	A/43
	29		Coys under Company arrangements. Wash'd cots food & shoes	A/45
	30		Coys under Company arrangements. Wash'd cots food & shoes.	S. O's were demobilised today.	A/45
	31		Coys under Company arrangements. H.R.H. The Prince of Wales visited Officers & men of the Battn unofficially. Wash'd cots food & shoes	S. O's demobilised	A/45

F. Mill Capt
Commanding 10th (S/Battn, The Royal Irish Rifles

Army Form C. 2118.

WAR DIARY
INTELLIGENCE SUMMARY
(Erase heading not required.)

Page 2.

Place	Date	Hour	Summary of Events and Information	Remarks and references to Appendices
MOUSCRON	1.2.19		Weather frosty. 2nd Lt. J.C. BREWSTER and 12 ORs proceeded to England to be demobilized.	cuts.
	2.2.19		Frost. Lieut C.A. KNIFTON, 2nd Lieut L.W. McALLISTER and 16 ORs proceeded to England for demobilization. Battalion attended Church Parade.	cuts.
	3.2.19		Frost. Capt. F.G. UPRICHARD and 20 ORs left battalion for demobilization.	cuts.
	4.2.19		Thaw during the day but frost during the night. 100 ORs were conveyed to LILLE on motor busses for the day.	cuts.
	5.2.19		Frost. Another party of 100 ORs proceeded to LILLE on busses for the day.	cuts.
	6.2.19		Frost. Lieut F. FARRELL, 2nd Lieut F.J. RUTTER M.C. and 9 ORs left the battalion for demobilization.	cuts.
	7.2.19		Frost. 18 ORs proceeded to England to be demobilized.	cuts
	8.2.19		Frost. 20 ORs proceeded to England to be demobilized.	cuts
	9.2.19		Frost. 240 ORs proceeded for demobilization.	cuts
	10.2.19		Frost. Lt. Col. W. McC. CROSBIE, D.S.O., rejoined the battalion from leave.	cuts.

WAR DIARY
INTELLIGENCE SUMMARY.
(Erase heading not required.)

Army Form C. 2118.

Page 1.

15 R I.F. Rifles
Vol 41

Place	Date	Hour	Summary of Events and Information	Remarks and references to Appendices
MOUSCRON	11.2.19		Inst. Ration Strength of battalion reduced to 15 Offs 394 ORs.	cuis.
	12.2.19		Inst. 2nd Lieut. W. LINTON and 38 ORs proceeded to England for demobilization	cuis.
	13.2.19		Inst. Capt. F.S. HILL, M.C. proceeded to the Concentration Camp LILLE for conducting duty. 35 ORs left the battalion for demobilization.	cuis.
	14.2.19		Inst. 32 ORs proceeded to England to be demobilized. Lieut. T. WALLACE. R.A.M.C. attd, proceeded to Concentration Camp, LILLE for conducting duty	cuis.
	16.2.19		Inst. 2nd Lieut. H.H. MC NEILL proceeded to Concentration Camp LILLE for conducting duty. 2nd Lieut R. INNIS. F.V.S. arrived to us in the final of the Annual Order Lip leaving the Battalion winners	cuis.
	16.2.19		Inst. Church Parade. 38 ORs proceeded for demobilization.	cuis.
	17.2.19		Inst. 40 ORs proceeded to England for demobilization	cuis.
	18.2.19		Ration Strength now 11 Offs and 230 ORs.	cuis.

WAR DIARY
INTELLIGENCE SUMMARY

Army Form C. 2118.
Page 3.

Place	Date	Hour	Summary of Events and Information	Remarks and references to Appendices
MOUSCRON	19.2.19	—	Ration strength 23 O.R. and 4 officers. Lieut. P.A. McIlwaine proceeds to XV. Corps H.Q. to act as Corps Courts Martial officer. Capt. Telfer M.C. returned from leave. Weather fine.	CWS.
"	20.2.19	—	11. O.R's demobilized ts-Say. Weather fine.	CWS.
"	21.2.19	—	12. O.R's demobilized ts-Say. Wet afternoon.	CWS.
"	22.2.19	—	46. O.R's demobilized ts-Say. 10 horses sent away ts-Say.	CWS.
"	23.2.19	—	100. O.R's and Captain L.S. Duncan. M.C. and Lt. J.H.O. McKEE transferred to 12.R. Irish Rifles to proceed to the army of occupation in Germany.	CWS.
"	24.2.19	—	2/Lt. L.S. Deverber proceed to England ts-Say for demobilisation. Weather fine. Ration strength 4 officers and 100. O.R's.	CWS.
"	25.2.19	—	Weather fine — Ration strength 4 officers 99. O.R's.	CWS.

Page 4. Army Form C. 2118.

WAR DIARY
INTELLIGENCE SUMMARY.
(Erase heading not required.)

Place	Date	Hour	Summary of Events and Information	Remarks and references to Appendices
Mouscron	26.2.19		Weather Fine. Ration Strength 9 Officers. 100 ORs.	AAA
	27.2.19		Weather Fine. 25 ORs transferred from 12th R. Irish Rifles to this Battn. for the purpose of demobilization as the 12th R. Ir. Rifles go to Germany on March 1st.	AAA
	28.2.19		Weather Showery. 2 ORs demobilized to-day — 12 horses and 1 mule demobilized to-day —	AAA

Wm. G. Prestone
Lieut. Col.
Comdg. 15th (S) Bn. The Royal Irish Rifles.

15 R Irish Rifles

Army Form C. 2118.

WAR DIARY
INTELLIGENCE SUMMARY.

(Erase heading not required)

Instructions regarding War Diaries and Intelligence Summaries are contained in F. S. Regs., Part II. and the Staff Manual respectively. Title pages will be prepared in manuscript.

Place	Date 1919 March	Hour	Summary of Events and Information	Remarks and references to Appendices
MOUSCRON (BELGIUM)	1st		Weather fine. 2 ORs demobilized to-day.	
"	2nd		Weather fine.	
"	3rd		Reported to-day that Lieut F. Farrell demobilized on 10th ult, died of influenza in BELFAST on 24th ult. 5 ORs demobilized to-day.	
"	4th		Major J.D.M. McCALLUM, D.S.O, returned from leave to the U.K.	
"	5th		Weather fine and warm. Ration Strength 108 ORs.	
"	6th		Fine day. Captain F.J. HILL, M.C, returned from leave.	
"	7th		Showery and cold. Lieut. T. WALLACE, R.A.M.C, (Att.) returned from leave.	
"	8th		Showery and cold. Major J.D.M. McCALLUM, D.S.O, Captain F.J. HILL, M.C, and Captain C.N.L. STRONGE, M.C, "B" reconnoitred the area AVELGHEM to ascertain amount of timber cut by the Germans.	
"	9th		26 ORs proceeded to England for demobilization, including Sgts. MACKIE, THORPE, McCULLOUGH and C.Q.M.S. WOODSIDE, who have re-enlisted and been finally approved in their rank. Ration Strength 8 Offs. 84 ORs.	
"	10th		Fine day. Sgt. Bugler BEHETS proceeded to-day to England for 3 months leave, having re-enlisted in the Royal Irish Rifles. Lieut. P.A. McELWAINE rejoined the Battalion from XV Corps H.Q. where he had been acting as Corps Court Martial officer	

J. H. Ruck Major
Commdg. 15th (S) Bn. Royal Irish Rifles

Army Form C. 2118.

WAR DIARY
INTELLIGENCE SUMMARY
(Erase heading not required.)

Instructions regarding War Diaries and Intelligence Summaries are contained in F. S. Regs., Part II. and the Staff Manual respectively. Title pages will be prepared in manuscript.

Place	Date	Hour	Summary of Events and Information	Remarks and references to Appendices
MOUSCRON (BELGIUM)	1919 MARCH 11th		Weather fine but cold.	1/19
	12th		Weather fine. Field Marshall Sir DOUGLAS HAIG visited the Division and said goodbye to Commanding Officers.	1/19
	13th		Fine day.	1/19
	14th		Weather fine.	2/19
	15th		Weather fine. Lieut. T. WALLACE. R.A.M.C. att., proceeded to Second Army H.Q. COLOGNE.	2/19
	16th		Weather fine. The Battalion Badminton Team played the Divisional Artillery. Result 5 games all 104-115 in favour of the Battalion.	1/19
	17th		4 Officers and 30 O.R's joined from 2nd Bn Royal Irish Rifles as their cadre proceeded home to-day. 2 horses and 13 mules were also taken over.	1/19
	18th		Weather fine. 19 mules were demobilized to-day.	1/19
	19th		Weather fine. 2 horses demobilized to-day.	7/19
	20th		Weather cold. Lieut. F.W. MARSHALL. M.C., proceeded home to-day for demobilization.	1/19

J. H. Lowry Major
Commdg. 15th(S) Bn. Royal Irish Rifles.

Army Form C. 2118.

WAR DIARY
INTELLIGENCE SUMMARY.
(Erase heading not required.)

Instructions regarding War Diaries and Intelligence Summaries are contained in F. S. Regs., Part II. and the Staff Manual respectively. Title pages will be prepared in manuscript.

Place	Date 1919 MARCH	Hour	Summary of Events and Information	Remarks and references to Appendices
MOUSCRON (BELGIUM)	21st		15 ORs transferred to 36th Bn. M.G. Corps to make up their cadre.	7/19
	22nd		22 ORs proceeded to demobilization Camp to-day.	7/19
	23rd		A/Capt. W.J. McDOWELL. M.C, and 2nd Lieut. H.H. McNEILL returned from leave.	7/19
	24th		Weather fine but cold.	7/19
	25th		Weather fine.	7/19
	26th		Weather cold.	7/19
	27th		1 OR proceeded to England for demobilization.	7/19
	28th		Lieut. H.E. MANN proceeded to the Demobilization Camp for dispersal. 1 OR transferred to the 36th Bn. M.G. Corps.	7/19
	29th		Lt. Col. W. McC. CROSBIE. D.S.O., Major J.D.M. McCALLUM. D.S.O., Lieut. W.J. McDOWELL. M.C., and 2nd Lieut. H.H. McNEILL proceeded to report to Second Army Headquarters.	7/19
	30th		Capt. C.N.L. STRONGE. M.C. proceeded on leave.	7/19
	31st		7 ORs proceeded for demobilization.	7/19

J. Hulsey Major.

Commdg., 15th (S) Bn. Royal Irish Rifles.

APRIL, 1919.

WAR DIARY
or
INTELLIGENCE SUMMARY.

1st R. Irish Rifles. Army Form C. 2118.

Place	Date	Hour	Summary of Events and Information.	Remarks and references to Appendices
MOUSCRON, BELGIUM.	1st			
	2nd			
	3rd			
	4th		Captain E.A. Telford M.C. & Lieut. J.B. Stevens & Lieut. A.J. Simpson proceed for demobilization	J.W.O
	5th		Lieut. P.A. McIldowie proceed for demobilization	J.W.O
	6th			
	7th			
	8th		Cr. W. Morris M.C. & proceed to join the B. army.	J.W.O
	9th			
	10th			
	11th			
	12th			
	13th			
	14th		Capt. J.J. Shin M.C. proceed on 14 days leave to U.K.	J.W.O
	15th			
	16th			
	17th		Lieut. P. Kelly rejoins from hospital.	J.W.O
	18th		Lieut. J.H. Davidson proceed for demobilization	J.W.O
	19th			
	20th			
	21st			
	22nd			
	23rd			
	24th		Lieut. C.B. Pippa returned from leave. 10. O.R's visited Ghent.	J.W.O
	25th			
	26th			
	27th			
	28th		10. O.R's visited Brussels.	J.W.O
	29th			
	30th			

30.4.1919.

J.H. Lury Major
Comdg. 15th (S) Bn. The Royal Irish Rifles.

Army Form C. 2118.

15 R Irish Rifles

WAR DIARY
or
~~INTELLIGENCE SUMMARY~~

(Erase heading not required.)

Instructions regarding War Diaries and Intelligence Summaries are contained in F. S. Regs., Part II. and the Staff Manual respectively. Title pages will be prepared in manuscript.

Place	Date	Hour	Summary of Events and Information	Remarks and references to Appendices
MOUSCRON BELGIUM	1.5.19			
	2.5.19			
	3.5.19			
	4.5.19			
	5.5.19			
	6.5.19	—	Lieut F.J. Ang proceeded on leave.	
	7.5.19			J.M.J.
	8.5.19	—	Lieut C.B. Pyfer and 7 ORs proceeded to England for demobilization.	J.M.J.
	9.5.19			
	10.5.19			
	11.5.19			
	12.5.19			
	13.5.19			
	14.5.19	—	Major T.H. Ivey D.S.O. proceeded on leave.	J.M.J.
	15.5.19	—	Capt F.J. Hill M.C. rejoined from leave.	J.M.J.
	16.5.19			
	17.5.19			
	18.5.19			
	19.5.19			
	20.5.19			
	21.5.19			
	22.5.19			
	23.5.19	—	Lieut J.J. O'Sullivan R.A.S.C. and 2 ORs joined from 1st Bn R.I. Rif. on the departure of that Battalions cadre for England.	J.M.J.
	24.5.19			
	25.5.19			
	26.5.19	—	Lieut F.J. Ang rejoined from leave. 10 ORs visited Ostend and Zebruge.	
	27.5.19			
	28.5.19			
	29.5.19	—	Major T.H. Ivey D.S.O. rejoined from leave.	J.M.
	30.5.19			
	31.5.19			

J.H. Ivey, Major
Commdg. 15th (S) Bn Royal Irish Rifles.

www.ingramcontent.com/pod-product-compliance
Lightning Source LLC
Chambersburg PA
CBHW081527160426
43191CB00011B/1705